rec read
June 6, 2021

# IN FINLAND

## YOU WOULD
## GET A TICKET FOR THAT

## MICHELLE L. PAIVOLA

ISBN: 978-1-09831-081-3

# PROLOGUE

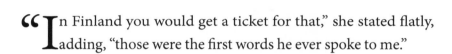

"In Finland you would get a ticket for that," she stated flatly, adding, "those were the first words he ever spoke to me."

The hospice nurse looked admiringly at the two of them as she pushed through the paperwork and continued asking questions. She was good at her job, humanizing those she helped to leave this life with as much dignity and as comfortably as possible.

"What?!" she asked with forced incredulity. "Sir, you can't criticize a woman's driving and expect her to fall in love with you." Her eyes twinkled with kindness.

"Well, he's an awesome kisser," the wife replied, a resigned hopelessness in her eyes and a deeper weariness in her voice. Their fingers were intertwined, their hands nestled in the hospital bed blankets. His bony and greyish hand rested on top of her living and pink flesh. He didn't say a word but looked apologetically into his woman's eyes, knowing the sorrow she would bear alone without him. But he could not carry on; not another step like this, not even for her.

The nurse grinned at them, "I'll bet he is," she continued, her pen traveling across the forms, marking the appropriate signature boxes. The wind howled around the rooftops of the hospital buildings; a tornado watch was in place and snow was in the forecast for the next day of this first week of April 2018. She observed that the best love stories had the most painful endings because of the agonizing, although temporary, separation. These two souls were still desperately clinging to one another but the silver cord was soon to snap. She knew it was infinitely better than those lonely beings that spent their last hours without anyone, or worse, with bitter, selfish family members arguing and hateful while they breathed their last breaths on their way into eternity.

"Alright, Mr. Paivola, the ambulance is scheduled to be here to take you home in about two hours. We will unhook you from everything except the NG tube and you can go home. One of our nurses will visit you tomorrow to make sure you're doing alright. Do you have any questions?"

They both shook their heads and she was dismissed without another word. She closed the door quietly as tears filled the wife's eyes and her face and composure began to crumple. He squeezed her hand with all the strength he was able to muster and he closed his eyes, his mind recalling moments with all those he loved. A wry smile crossed his worn out but still beautiful face as he relived those first moments with her nearly two decades ago.

# CHAPTER ONE

——⟨∞⟩——

"In Finland you would get a ticket for that," he stated brusquely in a thick British-English accent.

Michelle paused momentarily at his audacious insult. Her stormy green eyes widened, her nostrils flaring slightly, as she turned her Jeep Cherokee right on a red light, having failed to come to a complete stop first.

With her jaw clenched she gave a sideways glance towards her passenger and said, "Here, too, but there's no sign stating it is against the law and we are late." She had just picked up Lasse Paivola and his associate from their hotel where they had hardly had time to unload their suitcases after a delayed flight from Finland. Regardless, it was her task to gather the gentlemen and get them to her office to meet with the president of her company as well as the sales team.

The morning was already getting warm. August in Ohio becomes like a sauna; but that heat and humidity is what makes the corn grow. Michelle could feel tiny trails of sweat begin to tickle her skin under the pale pink business suit she was wearing as she led the way across the parking lot, blurry with heat waves, and into the cool air conditioning of the five story office building. Was she steaming from the inside or out? The two men followed her, speaking fervently in Finnish, while she silently fumed over this Lasse Paivola and the nerve he had to criticize her driving. But it wasn't just his words in the car; no, her animosity towards this man had started weeks ago before she even shook hands with him for the first time this morning.

The previous year Michelle had become the product manager of a Finnish-made communication system built for the public safety market. While her company was well-known for selling some of the best turnout gear for firefighters, bone conduction communication systems were difficult to grasp for the salesmen.

The supplying company from Finland was family owned and had grown overnight to more than they could handle. A headhunter had placed Lasse as the Managing Director and he had cleaned house in the four weeks he had taken over. Everyone hated the man. He had forced the owner to retire, fired his son, fired his son-in-law, fired one of their oldest sales reps, and was well on his way to firing the owner's daughter, a dear friend with whom Michelle was exchanging heated and colorful emails, all detailing their unified enmity towards Lasse. Michelle was at a low boil just thinking of the nerve of the man to fire everyone in a family owned company; and then he was so rude to come here and castigate her driving without having known her personally for five full minutes. The man perturbed her. What an ass; what an absolutely pompous ass. Who does this? Who does he think he is? He doesn't know these products or the family that started this company out of their garage, and he certainly doesn't care. Righteous indignation filled her. In Finland you would get a ticket for that. She would remember those words for all of eternity! His pretentious airs suffocated her behind her forced dignity at having to act as gracious host as she led the Finns through the maze of cubicles.

Michelle made several introductions and as she politely handed Lasse and his associate off to the president of the company, Jane, one of the accountants, whispered to her, "He is one good looking man."

Michelle looked bewilderedly at the woman and asked, "Which one?"

"The older one, the silver fox," she said, nodding towards Lasse who was wearing a navy silk suit and tie.

Michelle was confused by her comment. She had already formed such distaste for Lasse before she had ever laid eyes on the man that she failed to notice that he was actually quite beautiful. Lasse was six feet of lean European and he was masculine while most European men hinted of a more feminine side. His silvery-blonde hair was cut simply in a short Caesar style, parted on the left, and topped the face of a Viking. The piercing eyes were Prussian blue and they literally twinkled as he charmed people with his fluent bull shit. Once angered, though, his eyes became as icy as a Norwegian fjord and he could pin the boldest of men in their place with his glacier-like glare. His nose formed from a straight bridge making him look something like a statue of Hercules. It was perfectly straight and smooth but would curl more or less when he snarled. He held his mouth in a slightly mocking grin and his upper lip was a little less prominent than his slightly fuller bottom lip. The man's jaw was perfectly squared and clean shaven. Michelle had taken notice of none of this and for Lasse this must have been perplexing since all of his life he had been able to manipulate people with his beauty and charm. Her motto was, "pretty is as pretty does," and this guy was atrocious. She was ready to defend her Finnish friends whose company was being disemboweled by this so called silver fox. He was more like the fox in the hen house.

During the morning meetings in the conference room Lasse sat at the head of the table. Of course he did. The men in her company were mild-mannered and wanted to build a trusting cooperation with a reliable supplier. Lasse was out to destroy and then trample the residue. Michelle sat at the conference table to Lasse's left and silently evaluated his dreadful behavior. He ruled the boardroom and all acquiesced to his demands. "I want to see your sales figures for the last six months. If things are not satisfactory, then we will find a new American partner to be our master distributor," he threatened in a low, surly voice. He may as well have said he was going to make them an offer they couldn't refuse.

Michelle's boss nodded slowly, eyebrows raised, and looked down the length of the table while appearing to search his brain for some kind of response to this onslaught and replied steadily, "Okay, Lasse, we will get the sales figures to you." He raised his hands in an open gesture and looked Lasse straight into those icy blue eyes and continued, "I don't think anyone is ready to quit the good working relationship we have with your company in Finland. Our sales team is finding the products difficult to demo out in the field. With some training we could do a better job of selling the system."

Michelle had never witnessed someone so vehement in a business meeting. These were simple negotiations of a working partnership, not a war. Lasse's philosophy was to come out swinging, a kind of kick you in the balls and stomp on your face while you are down maneuver. He always hit first and asked questions later. This was one of the tactics he utilized to manipulate people to bend to his will. Her company was dedicated to selling the best equipment to the fire service and they, too, were a family owned company who had flourished in the one hundred years since they began. What the hell had just happened?

They broke for lunch and headed to a local restaurant. Lasse began to employ his charisma with the nephew of the owner of her company, who worked with Michelle. He was a gentle man, meek and kind, but purposeful in his endeavors to serve every day heroes who save others' lives. He didn't just help to compose the current company mission statement, he believed in it. He responded to Lasse's engaging words with chuckles and mellow enthusiasm. Michelle detested this game Lasse was playing with her bosses. To her he was obviously working all of them to achieve his own goals, which should have been in accord with theirs.

They placed their orders at the restaurant, and although the only woman, Michelle was not in the least uncomfortable. She was ambitious and a fighter, and having worked with men for the last five years, she had no qualms to share solutions and opinions with them. She was undaunted and purposeful. She had been raised in an orphanage, left there by her family when she was five years old, and then lived in a revolving door of foster homes. She was tough and street-smart and knew the smell of a bull shitter when she met one. She was a tall blonde with a curvy figure and a sharp wit that she rarely contained behind her disarming dimpled smile. Dark emerald formed a band around her almond-shaped green eyes; she was fierce all on her own. Hungry for respect and not for being desirable, the only thing she hated about working with men was that they did not seem capable of keeping their eyes off her large bosom; a curse that began in the third grade.

Looking around the table Michelle reluctantly noted that Lasse had impeccable table manners. His cuff-linked wrists supported perfectly groomed hands that held his knife and fork delicately as he focused on his meal. Unfortunately, the three other men, two Americans and one Finn, ate like ogres. Michelle observed as they stuffed far too much food into their gaping mouths, spoke while they were half chewing, and their teeth and lips were not always successful at keeping the masticated mess inside so that bits and small pieces escaped to the tablecloth. There was something different about Lasse; he was elegant but everything about him said he was dangerous. There was no doubt that he was powerful and the alpha male in any situation. How unfortunate that Michelle disliked him entirely.

The air conditioning was at full blast as Michelle pulled her Jeep out of the restaurant's parking lot when Lasse noticed her Finnish-English cassette tapes and translation book in the front dash.

"Who is trying to learn Finnish?" he inquired mockingly.

Darn it. Why hadn't she hidden those earlier? "I am," she replied tartly.

"Let me hear what you know," he demanded. All conversation paused in the car as the men waited for her to speak.

This man was abusive. Michelle gritted her teeth but spoke with confidence as she tilted her head slightly and said sweetly, "Missa hissi on?"

"In Finland they would laugh at you for saying it like that." What the hell? Really? Are you sure they wouldn't give me a ticket for that? Michelle thought indignantly but refrained from replying. Lasse could not be more offensive to her.

Seconds later Michelle's abhorrence rose to a new level as Lasse began cajoling the owner's nephew to come to Finland and to work for him. She was disgusted with him as he heaped piles of beautiful bull shit upon the men in the backseat while he openly criticized her. The man was absolutely preposterous!

Later that afternoon the negotiations ended well with the promise of training support for the salesmen, a new demo program, and an incentive program for sales quotas. It seemed that an inevitable fate had decided to test Michelle's mettle, pressing into her life this one man whom she could not ignore and who would change the course of her life forever.

# CHAPTER TWO

Michelle was in her early thirties and deeply involved in her life as a soon-to-be single mother of two boys. Michael was fourteen and Christopher was eleven; both very involved in sports at their school.

Having been a ward of the state during her childhood, Michelle was intent on being the best mother. It was not often she spoke of her childhood but her closest friends had heard fragments of her history. She didn't describe the abject misery and coldness of life in the orphanage or the shame and loss of a sense of value from being cast aside by her family. Her mother was an institutionalized paranoid schizophrenic who was incapable of caring for herself, let alone her children. The cruelties Michelle had lived through in the countless foster homes and at Parmadale Orphanage were not shared with anyone. Her first day at Parmadale, when her life was severed from her mother's, she had been playing on the porch of one of the house cottages when the house attendant told her, "Your mother is gone now and you are to live here." It was bluntly stated and there was no hug given with the delivery, no comfort given to that little blonde haired girl. There was no goodbye and no warning of being left behind. Michelle's heart was broken, her soul was shattered, cut so deeply, and sitting there in a t-shirt and shorts with children running all around her, she knew betrayal and learned abandonment. As her five year old mind comprehended her new situation, a silent wail caught in her throat and the tears poured from her soul. She hardened. She learned to rely on herself; she would be damned before she would ask help from anyone. And she learned that only Jesus loved her and could be trusted. In the last home she was raised in she was told, "You're not going to college, so pick something at the vocational school." When she inquired as to what she should pick, the reply was, "It doesn't matter what you pick; just pick anything." That was the level of concern for her future. She had always known she was on her own. These were the events that shaped her and yet, somehow she grew into a compassionate young woman. God had forged all that pain and sorrow into an unbreakable empath.

Michelle's sons had her full attention and devotion. She attended every practice and game her boys played in, and she applauded all their efforts. She watched over them like a hawk for fear that the tragedies and injustices that had been forced upon her would become the nightmare of her children suffering them as well. She came from a lifetime of trusting no one to becoming the doting mother with a stash of macaroni necklaces her little boys had bestowed upon her and boxes of every picture they had ever scribbled. She spent years on the floor with them playing with Legos. She loved her sons fiercely and encouraged them to be bold men. She taught them to give a firm handshake and look grownups directly in the eye by the time they were two years old. No one was going to take advantage of, use, or abuse her sons.

They lived in a small cottage on a five acre mini farm and had been blessed to have a retired thoroughbred who was more like a big dog than anything they dared to ride. Boodles Bay was nearing thirty years old and just enjoyed being brushed and fed apples, carrots, and treats. Michelle knew that her sons would learn responsibility by having animals to care for and she brought chickens, turkeys, sheep, pigs, and rabbits into their lives. When they were eight and five years old, she would order them to unload the feedbags of fifty pounds of grain. Whether they had to push it, pull it, drag it, or plop it from the Jeep into a wheelbarrow, it was their responsibility to get the bags into the barn. And they did. They found ways to get their jobs done and they grew stronger. Michelle said she didn't care if her boys loved her but they had better respect her. She loved them. She wanted the best for them but expected the best out of them.

Lasse had accepted the job with the small communications company after returning to Finland from having lived in Saudi Arabia for eight years. He had been a Second Lieutenant in the Finnish Army Reserves before he had begun his career in marine underwriting. He had traveled the world negotiating deals for hundreds of millions of dollars. He knew how to buy, sell, trade, steal, and force an unfavorable deal when needed. He was in his mid-forties when the Finnish government had offered him a job as a commercial counselor working at the Finnish Embassy in Saudi Arabia. He had spent eight years in that god-forsaken desert and it had cost him more than he wished he had been willing to pay. His children were now grown adults, all living on their own in Finland and he missed them. They had visited over the years but it wasn't the equivalent to living in the same city with them as he had when they were small and had been divorced from their mother. Marianne, his oldest and only daughter was married; Jere, his oldest son was also happily married; and Lauri had finally left home and was on his own as well. Lasse had come back to Finland in his early fifties and was a stranger to his second wife, as well as his homeland.

Lasse had been born less than a decade after World War II. His family was not the only one fighting for survival in the harsh land that is Finland. Sweden, the United States, and other neighboring countries had turned their backs on Finland as Russia invaded and Nazi Germany alone helped to fight off Stalin's attacks. Finland was the only European country to pay back all of their war debts and that meant hungry people who worked very hard. Lasse was the toughest of the tough; nothing and no one could beat him. His childhood had caused a resolve and determination in him that wouldn't allow defeat; he had an indomitable will.

He didn't mind being alone. He had been alone almost all of his life. His sister, Ritva, who was a year older than Lasse and his best friend, died from scarlet fever when he was thirteen. He and his little sister, Marjukka who was just four years old at the time, had little opportunity to grieve her loss. The Christmas that he was twelve years old, Ritva had given him a small New Testament that he carried with him all of his life. His parents were good, hard-working people but times were so hard and even before he attended the first grade, Lasse was working in the sugar beet fields for pay. It was more than a necessity for that little boy to work; his family's survival depended on it. They were so poor that Lasse often went to school without socks or shoes. He, too, had met with the cruelty of teachers using him as an example before the classroom, mocking him for being poverty-stricken and berating his father for circumstances beyond his control. That little boy also hardened and vowed he would do whatever it took to overcome; he would not be poor or ridiculed. When Lasse was only fourteen years old, he left for sea as a merchant sailor. He was a big, strong boy but even so, the work pushed him near to his limits and he was exhausted. He would return from voyages with huge sacks of sugar and coffee for his family and money to help them survive. He was beautiful at fourteen and learned to ask for love in every language of every port those ships carried him. He had the adventures every young man dreams of and escaped many bad situations but not without scars. He had been shot twice, stabbed multiple times, beaten with a baseball bat, and nearly drowned at sea on countless occasions. He had been drunken times without number before forsaking alcohol, chased by jealous husbands, and smuggled such a variety of goods – but never people or drugs. He hadn't been such a bad pirate. By the time he was eighteen he had enough wisdom to know he wasn't going to spend the rest of his life loading and unloading goods onto ships, and walking the docks looking for love and just hoping for a better life. He hiked all over Helsinki and filled out applications in every company with an open door. He was diligent in working in the mailroom of Pohjola Insurance Company, the largest in Finland; a company where two decades later he would become a vice-president. He rented one room in a boarding house, ate cheese sandwiches and afforded himself a slice of ham once a week; and he survived. He could envision his success, see himself in better circumstances, and he pushed himself up every hill. He enrolled himself in night school, earning his high school diploma, his Bachelor's degree, and later his Master's degree in Business Administration. He joined the Finnish Army Reserves and completed officer's training. In his early thirties he purchased a small farm for his parents; the first home of their own they had ever lived in. He traveled the world working in marine underwriting and rarely found himself for more than a week's time in Finland. Yes, he was always alone but where was home anyway? Nowhere felt like home and he belonged to no one. He thrilled at the adventures and dangers of working for the Finnish government that took him into countries like Tunisia, Afghanistan, and all over North Africa.

He retired from his work in Saudi Arabia and moved back to Finland. He spent the first three weeks playing golf with people he hadn't seen in nearly a decade. It didn't take long for him to need more in his life than eighteen holes and lunch at the country club. He always needed a challenge and so when the headhunter called with the opportunity to manage the small communications company, he gladly accepted.

The company was in a shambles with creditors demanding payment, the owner's kids taking advantage of the profits; it was a mess. He would whip and conquer that company into shape and prepare it to be sold to one of the largest investment conglomerates in Finland. On his first visit to the office, before he had actually accepted the position, no one was available to take a call from an irate supplier of components. Lasse was handed the phone and listened while a screaming woman demanded payment for the goods she had supplied months earlier. She swore and degraded his mother's good reputation and the origin of his birth. He said, "Ma'am, I don't work here but I will see to it that you are paid promptly."

This was just the kind of challenge he required. Before long he had forced resignations of insolent loafers, sliding their resignation papers slowly across the table towards them. When they baulked at having to leave he would state coldly and quietly, "Don't fuck with me," and piercing them with his icy blue eyes threaten, "and I won't fuck with you." They always signed and left right away.

Lasse did everything intensely. Whatever he endeavored he did with full force. He had never been bored in his life and he always achieved his objective. He was tenacious and he didn't waste time.

# CHAPTER THREE

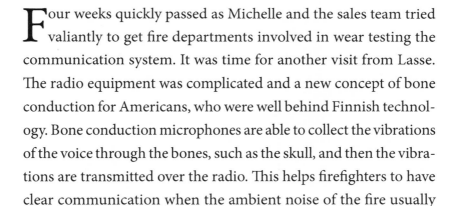

Four weeks quickly passed as Michelle and the sales team tried valiantly to get fire departments involved in wear testing the communication system. It was time for another visit from Lasse. The radio equipment was complicated and a new concept of bone conduction for Americans, who were well behind Finnish technology. Bone conduction microphones are able to collect the vibrations of the voice through the bones, such as the skull, and then the vibrations are transmitted over the radio. This helps firefighters to have clear communication when the ambient noise of the fire usually drowns out their voices.

Lasse flew to Ohio to oversee his Finnish associate's training of Michelle's sales team. It was a two day event in which she behaved politely towards him but remained aloof. The word from her friend in Finland was that Lasse was searching for another company to be the American master distributor and he was going to build his own sales force in the States.

Lasse's next visit to the States was a couple of months later to attend an international fire fighter trade show and conference held in Indiana. Michelle saw Lasse from a distance as he approached his own small sales team, which included his original Finnish associate, a big old country boy from Alabama, and a slick Hispanic guy from San Diego. He wasn't shouting, he never shouted, but he was certainly snarling at them. What a jerk, she thought. In Lasse's defense that sales team was losing his company $200,000 annually; they had well overspent at the previous night's dinner and drinking, had rented the most expensive hotel for the week, and could not produce the leads generated for the past two days of the trade show. Of course, Michelle did not know any of this but she thought it prudent to avoid Lasse at that time, especially without having any encouraging results of her own to report. He had remained neutral towards her cold indifference. He was as polite as she was but neither of them was warming towards the other.

Lasse visited the States again another six weeks later because he believed people do what it is inspected, not expected. He was in Ohio to review the outcome of the wear tests from the fire departments and to see if the sales had increased following the trade show. Michelle had nothing much to report and while that was disheartening, she truly believed that was going to turn around. She was street-tough but also blindly optimistic; she always found the silver lining in any grey cloud.

Michelle's boss wasn't accustomed to suppliers making such an intense inspection of his company's sales efforts. The Finn made him uncomfortable and he passed him off to Michelle. "Lasse, Michelle is going to show you our newly installed software program to track our customer relationship management," he stated as he quickly walked away. She had only had one training on the program but her motto was, "fake it until you make it," and that is just what she did with Lasse looking over her shoulder. He surely knew a bull shitter while listening to her pretend to understand that program. The man had written computer programs for companies in Saudi Arabia from his own small business. He knew and it annoyed him to be wasting time with this. He expected sales results and he wasn't getting them.

After six months it was evident to Michelle's company that this product was not a good fit for them. It was too high-tech for the sales team. The top salesman, Jonah Weaver, came to see her and said frankly, "Look, we can't sell that product because we don't know anything about radios. We measure and outfit people in turn-out gear. We can go in and sell a thousand sets of turnout gear in an afternoon. It is taking months for these wear tests and we don't know how to answer the questions about radio frequencies. We don't know anything about radios. That's it." It finally made sense to her.

Michelle was grateful for Weaver's candor. "Thanks, Brother; I get it. It's never going to work and that's not your fault. This product is just not a good fit for us."

Michelle began to calculate what was going to be done with the half million dollars of Finnish made communication equipment they had in their inventory at the company's distribution facility. She sent an email to Lasse's Finnish associate who was living in San Diego and much easier to deal with, asking what the restocking fee would be for the return of their products. She provided part numbers and quantities in a spreadsheet and emailed it off to the West Coast. Within minutes Lasse, who was in Finland, gave her a call. He was seven hours ahead of Eastern Standard Time and it was nearing 10pm in Finland.

"What is this about a restocking fee, Michelle? We don't take returns."

"Of course you take returns, Lasse. We just want to know what the restocking fee is and how we can go about getting your products back to you."

"How many units do you want to return?" he demanded.

"Didn't your associate tell you? I emailed the spreadsheet to him just a little while ago."

"How many units do you want to return? I didn't ask him, I am asking you."

"You'll have to get the spreadsheet from him. He is my direct contact and he has the answer to your question." There was no way Michelle was going to tell Lasse she intended to return all of his products. She didn't have that kind of courage and she was sure that he already knew the answer.

Lasse's voice turned harder and quieter than it already was and he said, "What kind of office politics are you trying to play with me? I want to know how many units you are requesting to return."

Michelle steeled her own reserve against his ferocious bullying, as this Finn was growling in her ear. She retorted slowly and concisely, "I told you, you will have to get that information from your associate." Both of them pissed off, they simultaneously hung up their phones and fumed over the obstinate beast they had just been talking with; only Michelle had tears of frustration.

She walked across the office to her boss' cubicle and declared, "I hate that guy."

"What happened? What did he say?" was his eager inquiry. How nice of him to hide in his cubicle while sending her to the Finnish wolves.

"He demanded to know how many units we want to return and I told him to get it from San Diego!" She chuckled nervously as she swiped a tear from her face. Never had she cried at work. Never had anyone gotten under her skin like this Lasse Paivola.

Lasse had his own words for women or men who wouldn't meet his demands. He was alone and shouted one of them while taking his work-booted foot to the stainless steel trash can, kicking a dent into the side. That woman was ridiculously infuriating. And that company had not produced any profits over the last six months. This was no way for any company to achieve sales goals and the American partner was not putting forth the effort needed to sell this product in the most profitable target market. They were getting a deadline and an ultimatum.

Three weeks later Michelle was in a heated telephone conversation with her sister, Heather. "I'm just saying I cannot possibly drive three hours into the hills of Kentucky with this man. I can't do it. What in the hell am I going to talk about with him for three hours?" she shouted.

"Michelle, do not get into a fight with this man! Talk about the weather, talk about anything other than work!" Heather advised.

Michelle sighed with exasperation. "You don't understand; I cannot simply talk about the weather with him! I hate his guts! I cannot stand him, Heather. They are making me take him for a tour of the distribution center in the middle of nowhere Kentucky. Three hours there and three hours back. And why? Because they don't want to face him in the office again! They are sending me out with him as a lamb for slaughter! He has fired everyone; nobody likes him in Finland or here. He is an asshole. I was the one who had to tell him we want to return half a million dollars of his product and he is pissed off with me."

"Well, I'll pray for you, Sister, but you need to calm down. Just be nice."

"Oh, my gosh," Michelle said with exasperation, "that's right, Heather, you don't understand, but please do pray for me."

It was the end of March and still quite chilly in Ohio the morning that Michelle picked up Lasse from his hotel which was nearby her office. The company had arranged for one of the customer service reps to go along for the ride; quite possibly they felt guilty for sending Michelle out like a sacrifice. James was the funniest, nicest, and most interesting guy and he was also morbidly obese. Michelle fretted because she did not want to embarrass him but she knew he was going to have to ride shotgun and Lasse, their guest, was going to have to ride in the backseat. There was no way Michelle would cause humiliation to anyone on purpose. She also followed proper etiquette and protocol at every turn but there was nothing to do but pick Lasse up and explain the situation to him. It grated against her pride to be put into a position where she had to humble herself and ask this man for help; but it was for the benefit of her coworker and friend.

"Good morning, Sir," she stated formally.

"Good morning, Ma'am," Lasse returned in a deep voice. Good morning indeed, he thought sullenly, calculating the cost of his trip to the States to once again be put off his objective.

"Listen, I would never say a bad word about anyone but the guy who is going with us to the distribution center is not going to fit into my backseat. Would you mind to ride back there and we won't say anything about it?"

"Not a problem; I am happy to ride in the back." Back or front, what did it matter? This was a waste of time and money as this company did not have the knowledge or drive to be the master distributor of the Finnish communication system. He contemplated the end of the cooperation with these Americans as there would be no ultimatum given. It was over.

"Thank you so much." She was sincerely grateful but found that Lasse sat himself in direct view of her rearview mirror. His fierce blue eyes were continually meeting her green eyes and it aggravated her. How annoying, she thought and shoved her sunglasses on to avoid further eye contact.

They pulled into the parking lot of her office and James loaded himself into the front seat. It took three tries to get the door closed but once all three were ensconced, James' happy demeanor and vast knowledge of a variety of subjects filled the vehicle with at least a measure of peace.

"I need to make a stop," Lasse announced.

Not sure what he needed and where to stop, Michelle asked, "Do you need something to eat?"

"No," he replied solemnly without further explanation.

"Do you need a rest area, a bathroom?" In the United States you may have any number of options to meet any kind of need. Michelle pulled off her sunglasses and looked back at Lasse in her rearview mirror with raised eyebrows.

"No."

What the hell did the man want? "Why do you need to stop?" Lasse's eyes caught Michelle's widened and questioning eyes in her mirror.

"I need a cigarette break," he answered curtly. His resolution to behave decently would require high doses of nicotine delivered to his nervous system. He could snap her neck in less than five seconds; the man of great substance, however, might require a bit more effort. Lasse was at a low boil. He had spent all of the prior day traveling half way across the world, only to be tossed into the back of this Jeep and forced to ride to southern Kentucky on a ruse. This journey had no meaning whatsoever to him and his agenda. He was frustrated to be diverted from his target and a good, long smoke would soothe his nerves.

"Oh." Michelle paused, relaying a slightly judgmental tone with an elongated stare. "Okay, just give me a few minutes," she said as she looked for an exit with a fast food restaurant.

James went in for a mid-morning snack while Michelle talked about the weather and Ohio with Lasse during his cigarette break. Of course he found her attractive but this was business. She was tough but didn't have any higher education. She had the balls to fly by the seat of her pants and push a team of people to sell a product he knew very well was difficult and complicated. Regardless, Lasse was still exasperated with these lazy Americans who didn't have the drive to equip their public safety personnel with better communication. He didn't look forward to ending this cooperation but it had to be done. He squinted in the morning sunshine, took a last pull of his cigarette, and muttered, "In Finland this would be a warm summer day."

Michelle couldn't help but chuckle infectiously and her smile deepened her dimples and reached all the way to her eyes. Finally a breakthrough to the ice queen's heart; smiling back at Michelle, he found that his own frozen Finnish heart had warmed towards her as well. He had to admire her tenacity; and her figure.

The tour of the distribution center was interesting and efficient enough but had nothing whatsoever to do with selling the Finnish made communication equipment. Lasse asked several questions and Michelle quietly observed the man. He was polite, interested, engaged, and even charming with everyone. She realized that her company was wasting this man's time and his company's money. She was ordered to take him as far away from the office as possible because they didn't know how to face him. Who wouldn't be pissed off with that treatment? Of course, she understood their hesitation when things were going so badly. And yet, he was gracious and charmed everyone in the Kentucky facility. He was especially favored by the women who whispered about his extraordinary good looks as he passed by them smiling and nodding a "Good morning, ladies," delivered in his deep, sexy European accent and his blue eyes twinkling. Michelle hadn't noticed that she was doing the same; her own behavior mirrored that of Lasse's. They could have been a noble couple bestowing gracious greetings to a devoted people.

Before they left the facility Lasse bent over to pick up a dropped file folder. His trousers stretched tautly against his muscled backside and for the first time Michelle noticed him as a physically attractive man. Nice ass, she thought. What? Her mind argued. You can't think that about him. Just stating the obvious. Well, don't.

The three hours in the Jeep on the way back to the office were filled with conversation about different genres of music that James enjoyed and Lasse knew, which did not include much but James tried. The last stop of the afternoon was in West Chester, Ohio, about 40 minutes south of the office. Michelle pulled into a Wendy's restaurant and James ambled in for a snack. Lasse stood on the curb and began to explain the direction that he was taking his company to Michelle.

"It's just business, it is nothing personal. It is important that we make money and that isn't going to include you or your company any longer," Lasse said directly as he extracted a cigarette from his nearly empty Marlboro pack.

Michelle nodded and said, "Yeah, I get it. Our salesmen outfit people in turnout gear and they don't know anything about radios. To me it isn't just business, though. It is very personal, as it always should be because you're dealing with people and relationships, but thank you for being forthright with me, Sir."

This was disappointing news but she understood and was grateful that he bothered to explain. The fight was over. She shivered in her black business suit as the cold March afternoon turned cloudy. Lasse had just lit his cigarette but put it out as he said, "You're freezing, let's go."

And it was at that very moment her soul recognized him. No one in her entire life had ever cared if she was cold, or hungry, hurt, or lost. It was a simple, kind gesture. It occurred to her like a whisper from God above that he wasn't such a bad guy after all. If her life had been any different, more benevolent, less severe, Michelle's soul never would have recognized Lasse's soul. If she had turned left instead of right, or chosen a different career path, they never would have met; it was as if a sacred convergence was the catalyst for every decision she had ever made. He hadn't touched her, made any vulgar or suggestive comments, and hadn't been caught ogling her breasts. He had been patient and willing to help her to understand. He had offered kindness that was foreign to her. And although the air was chilly, she was warmed as she reevaluated this Lasse Paivola.

The next morning was Saturday but Lasse had asked if Michelle could take him to the airport for his flight back to Finland. The man was accustomed to asking favors from everyone, promising payment by way of strawberry milkshakes, which he never delivered. His requests were always willingly met; people liked helping that man. "Ask and ye shall receive," was Lasse's motto.

"Sure, why not?" Michelle agreed. So the arrangements were made and a map was consulted as this was an airport in Columbus where Michelle had never been and was almost two hours from her home.

When she picked Lasse up he wasn't wearing his typical navy silk or grey wool suit with pinstriped shirt and cufflinks. He was wearing a light grey sweatshirt, jeans, and a pair of Timberland boots that made him look more relaxed but none the less dangerous. Silver fox for sure, Michelle thought. Good grief, he was actually very attractive. Good heavens and she was going to drive this man all the way to Columbus. How had she only just noticed how gorgeous he was?

"Good morning!" she beamed. She was an absolute ray of sunshine on the cold and dismal March morning, dressed in jeans, sneakers, and a black Nike track jacket.

"Good morning, Ma'am! How are you today?" he asked admiring her dimples and finding it hard not to return the sparkle in her green eyes that reminded him of the sea when the sunshine hits it. She was genuine, full of passion, and she put her heart and soul into whatever she was doing. She was adorable and adored by her coworkers, including all of the Finnish team. She had that certain quality, the ability to automatically care for others, which made people fall in love with her – men, women, children, even people who hated her ended up loving her. And as Lasse noted all her attributes, he thought she certainly was voluptuous; a real Marilyn Monroe in his book.

"If I was six months younger...." he muttered under his breath.

"What?!" Michelle had heard him, as he intended. She faked a seething sideways glance at him but consulted the map making sure of the exit she needed before they even left the parking lot.

What was he thinking? She was twenty years younger than he was but there was something about this young woman that drew him. He had been alone for a very long time, years in fact. What the hell? It was just a fun comment and he knew he still had what it took to lure any woman. Besides, he was never going to see her again after today. There wasn't much to do but sort out who got the china and who got the silver once their companies parted ways. He wondered if she would remember him with any forgiveness for creating such calamity to her professional life as he climbed into the front seat of her Jeep.

After much discussion about Finland and Michelle's common Finnish heritage during the hour and a half drive, Lasse asked, "Are we getting close? We don't have much more time before boarding begins. Is the airport near?"

"Uh, yeah, I think so," Michelle replied, not really sure. "The map says it should be here somewhere. Do you see any signs for an airport? I've never actually been to this airport in Columbus." She turned the map first one way and then the other while keeping her Jeep at the very least on her side of the highway. He wondered how she had managed to stay alive during her years of driving. God's grace, he imagined.

"I don't see any airplanes coming and going; we should see planes. What is the address you have there?"

"Uh, it says Columbus Municipal Airport."

"We want the International Airport. Do you know where that is?"

"Uh, no, I guess not," she admitted hesitantly.

"Okay, well," he paused, "let me look at your map." He searched until he found the right location and exits. Michelle followed his orders and as they were nearing his flight's boarding time she increased her speed, her green eyes constantly darting to the clock on the dash. If this had been a weekday, there would have been no way to arrive in time for his flight.

"Oh my gosh, Lasse, I am so sorry!" she exclaimed as she pulled right up to the departures entry doors.

"No worries, Ma'am!" he shouted as he opened up the back of her Jeep, grabbed his bag, and started sprinting for the door. But an intuitive urgency told him to turn around. She stood there smiling and waving as he left, even though in reality he had fired her. He paused to look at her. This would be the last time he would see this vivacious, beautiful, sweet girl. He put his bag down, hurriedly stepped back towards her, and tugged her into his arms in what turned out to be a galvanizing and unforgettable hug. It was at that moment, at that very moment Lasse was willing to try, six months younger or not. In all of his life and worldly travels he had never met a woman like her. He admired her fierce goodness and determination. She was genuine and beautiful inside and out. He considered pensively if she was the reason fate had brought him to the middle of nowhere Ohio. He determined then that she was going to be his.

# CHAPTER FOUR

During the following months Michelle's job took her into the international supply chain once again. She had a charm that made the Germans swoon, as now she was importing and selling German-made leather firefighter boots. She had fortitude and determination that had been forged for lack of the opportunities that others had squandered. She wrote user guides and had them published, set up shoe repair shops, and conducted trainings making sure her sales team knew it was "all about boots". She fought the competition publically when they tried to disparage her supplier's quality and safety. She loved every minute of the challenges. She was a fighter and maybe she, too, knew how to kick them in the balls and stomp on their faces while they were down. She could certainly take the hits and come back fighting.

Jonah Weaver stopped by her desk on his way out and congratulated her on a job well done, giving her a thumbs up and announcing that it was "all about boots". She admired him, his kindness, and the way he had in guiding people with encouragement. She had been blessed with good people in her life.

And yet, she still wanted to work with the communication equipment. Michelle had written to Lasse the week he returned to Finland asking him to consider her as the master distributor. She knew the product and she knew the dealers, and she had the customers in at least 4,000 fire departments across the United States. It was a bold suggestion but she had the confidence that she could train the dealers and make a success of this product in the United States' public safety market. He wanted an established company with a sales force to take control of selling the product and a two-way radio company in San Diego was ready to sign a contract. So, she let go of wanting to work with the Finnish company and moved on with her work life, setting new goals with the Germans. She had submitted the idea that in lieu of a restocking fee with the Finnish supplier, her company could sell the equipment to the new master distributor in San Diego at cost and everyone would win. Lasse accepted that, her company agreed, and the new distributer was willing to buy all the stock.

During her first year as the product manager of the German-made leather firefighting boots, the sales were just shy of a million dollars. She was happy with her accomplishments and planning for more. The German company was thrilled with her company's efforts and with Michelle's dedication.

That summer Michelle joined a group of her girlfriends and headed out West for a trip to Montana. Grown women giggled like school girls, looped arms, sang camp songs, ate like men, and for the first time in her life she was invited to a sauna.

The moms and sisters and grandmothers hiked miles up the Bitterroot Range of the Rocky Mountains to Bear Creek Overlook. Michelle had always been one for safety but she joined her girlfriends as they crawled halfway out over a ledge on their bellies that overlooked the most amazing valley; trees and cliffs and clouds all beneath her. She held her arms out over the expanse and the rush of cold air that came up made it feel as if she was flying, her blonde hair blowing up behind her. Something in her life had changed but she didn't have the understanding of it yet.

Later, she was alone with her Bible beside one of the creeks at an old grist mill that had been converted to a guest house. She sat quietly under the birch trees on a large, flat rock and listened to the sounds of the wild Montana wilderness. The creek was tumultuous as it rushed down from the mountains; its supply was melted snow that was still icy and clean. Upstream the water had white caps from the force but downstream she could see where it became quiet and traveled almost sleepily through the rays of sunshine that illuminated the rocks in the creek bed. From there the water took a turn around a bend and she could not see where it went. She wrote in her journal the words that God spoke to her innermost being. *Your life is like this creek. There are times when things will be rough as you navigate over rocks and rush forward, but then you will have peaceful times. You will go around corners and you will not know where they will lead. And that is how your life will be but I am with you.* She returned from that June trip refreshed and more certain of herself than ever. Her life was changing but she would not walk alone through any of it.

# CHAPTER FIVE

❧

It was the middle of July and nearing five months since Lasse had replied to Michelle. He hadn't heard from her since her email asking him to consider her offer to be the master distributor, but he hadn't forgotten her for one moment either. She was his objective. He sent her an email inviting her to Salt Lake City to help him with a trade show. She sent a sassy reply that it was his tough luck to have fired everyone. Smiling at her audacity, he dropped his dog tags from between his lips that he always wore on a silver chain around his neck, and sent a reply email asking her to help him out. He would pay her for the week, and she could stay in the best hotel in Salt Lake City. Her stomach got little butterflies as she told him she would do it and set up a week's vacation with her company.

As Michelle stood at the outside check-in at the airport in Columbus, the same place she had shared the unforgettable hug with Lasse, the wind was hot and the air was humid. It was August, a year since the first time she had shaken hands with Lasse Paivola. She had taken great care in choosing this dress, a black summer suit with a pencil skirt and polka-dot sleeveless top with a square neckline that showed no cleavage. She was tanned and toned from summer days at the pool with her boys and she wore kitten heeled, black strappy sandals, and a simple diamond necklace and stud earrings. Her blonde hair was a little longer but layered to frame her face. She was pretty but modest and wore her sunny disposition over her fiery, passionate personality.

The guy working at the flight check-in counter looked her over and stated words that may as well have been a long, low wolf whistle, "He is one lucky guy."

"Yes, he is," Michelle stated as a matter of fact but then shared a chuckle with the man. Her entire life she had been used to men perusing her. She ignored it and held her head up high. She hadn't used her physical assets for any gain or glory but neither was she ashamed of herself.

Lasse was waiting for Michelle at the airport in Salt Lake City. He wasn't nervous; he was purposeful. Dear God, she was beautiful, he thought as he waited for her. Every time he had seen her that was the prevailing thought. She knew it but never flaunted her beauty, always demanding respect without having to say so. Lasse was dressed in casual navy pants and a blue pinstripe button-down shirt he knew complimented his eyes. But he had made a serious change in growing a mustache and goatee. Hell, even he thought he looked sexy.

Holy smokes, he thought as she came through the gate to the baggage claim. Her blonde hair was strikingly bright against her strong, tan limbs, as she took long, slow strides through the arrival gate. He sauntered up to her, not rushing, but relishing the moment she saw him. He knew he was beautiful and that the new facial hair had brought desired looks from all the women he came in contact with. It was a change he had made because he was about to transform his life forever.

"Hi!" she said happily, looking like sunshine to his grey and lonely life. She was spunky and well-mannered, not too cool but neither was she falling all over him. She had never said one suggestive word to him, nor had she indicated that she was interested in him physically. But Lasse had a sense that they would be together and he was putting forth all his effort to make that happen.

"Hello, Ma'am," he said in a deep voice and he grabbed her in a polite, friendly hug. She was gorgeous and she smelled like delicious vanilla sugar.

Lord have mercy, Michelle thought, and the butterflies in her stomach were fully engaged as he held her body tightly to his in the brief hug. Lasse Paivola was the sexiest man alive. His accented voice was deep and rich, and with that new goatee, she found it hard to be aloof and keep her mind on the business conversation they were having. The blue stripe in his shirt electrified the blue of his eyes or perhaps it was the space between them that was charged. His lips were framed by the new silver whiskers and he looked dangerously close to devouring her, all the while discussing the trade show events as if the undercurrents of desire between them weren't present.

He pulled her suitcase along as they traveled on the pedestrian walkway but with all his heart he hoped to win her affections. Lasse had been twice married, he had been dedicated and faithful in his relationships, he had carried a flame for his first love for thirty years, a girl he had loved before either of his wives came into his life. But Michelle, Michelle was different from any woman he had ever loved. She was kind and yet a fighter, she was good and wholesome and not selfish; she also possessed a tenacity the Finns referred to as sisu. They had different personalities but shared the same fervor, goodness, and passion for life. He was in love with this woman and nothing and nobody was going to separate them. Neither of them was perfect, but they were perfect for each other.

The Grand America Hotel in Salt Lake City was elaborate. Lasse wanted to impress Michelle and had arranged for her to have an executive suite in this five diamond hotel with a view of the Wasatch Range, part of the Rocky Mountains. With her love of the Rockies, he could not have been guided to a better selection. He helped her with the check-in and handed her room keys to her. They agreed to meet in the lobby in an hour after she settled in, to go for a walk to stretch her legs after her long flight from Ohio.

When Michelle entered her room, she was captivated with the beauty of the mountains and the suite itself. She looked at her reflection in the mirror of the marbled bathroom and yet it was Lasse's blue eyes that she kept seeing. Oh my gosh, she kept saying to herself, that man is beautiful and powerful and he wants me. She had never been more attracted to anyone. She hugged herself, smiling, and flopped herself down on the bed. She could not have been more happily excited. She closed her eyes and created a mental memory of Lasse to be stored in her heart for the rest of forever.

Having changed into a more suitable walking outfit of khaki shorts, a white t-shirt, and sneakers, Michelle made her way to the lobby. The elevator door resonated with a perky bing and the doors silently parted. And there he was, staring at her as if he would consume her at that moment. Lasse grabbed Michelle's hand and quickly led her out the glass front doors into the warm August afternoon air. Both of them silently shared a giddy expectancy of falling madly in love with each other as their fingers interlocked automatically, as if they had done it thousands of times earlier instead of for the first time that day.

The atmosphere was hot as they strolled down sidewalks across the city, sharing their life histories and listening intently to each other. Lasse teased Michelle by asking, "Why is your hand sweating in mine? Do I make you nervous?"

Michelle threw her head back and laughed loudly, replying, "No, Sir, your hand is the one sweating because I make you nervous!" He squeezed her hand tightly and their souls were intertwined, not just their fingers.

Lasse led Michelle into a shaded park at the Salt Lake City and County Building. It was cooler there and the building perched behind them was made of granite and elaborately carved in grey sandstone; solid like the fortress they were discovering in their relationship, something that felt as if it was being excavated from ancient days.

Lasse turned towards Michelle on the park bench and asked, "Are those real diamonds you're wearing? Because I am a poor man and I can't afford anything like that." She cracked up and shook her head, but within she understood that Lasse wanted to be loved for the man he was and not for any earthly baubles he could or could not bestow.

"No problem, Sir, I am not in need of diamond earrings!" Her heart adored him. That was all. Neither of them questioned this awareness that they had merged and would walk through life together from now on. It hadn't even been stated; it didn't need to be.

They returned to their rooms at the Grand America and Michelle soaked in a huge tub full of bubbles and grinned continuously while thanking God for this amazing man. He was better than any romance novel hero she had ever read or could have fantasized about; reality was better than her dreams. From then on she would always regard him with awe. She put on a light summer dress and sandals, her blonde hair falling past her shoulders, and headed to the lobby to meet Lasse for dinner, a smile permanently fixed upon her face.

He took her hand in his again as they walked to dinner at Absolute!, a local Swedish restaurant. Michelle studied the menu the best that she could while Lasse studied her intently, eating her up with his piercing blue eyes. She couldn't focus. Now he was making her nervous but she wasn't afraid of him. He excited her, like a match that had been struck to finally light the wick of the candle of her being. Lasse brought life and breath to Michelle's soul. She imagined that it was like the moment Eve took her first breath and Adam took her hand and showed her all the beautiful things in the Garden of Eden. It was like the first day of life for her. All that had happened before was nothing and forgotten, however necessary it was to arrive at this moment.

Lasse could not stop staring at Michelle. She finally said, "If you want me to eat this dinner then you need to stop looking at me like that."

"Like what?" he said huskily in that accent that made men and women turn their heads whenever he spoke.

"Like you are going to eat me for supper! Stop it please." But he could not help himself. For Lasse it was as if an angel had been placed before him. She was the sweetest, most brilliant being and he could not look away from the light that shown through her. Whatever their meals consisted of was irrelevant; they drank in the essence of each other's souls and the other was all that mattered any longer. They had each found the one whom their souls loved and they would now experience the joy and agony of true devotion.

Lasse held tightly to Michelle's hand as he walked her back up the darkened but still busy streets of Salt Lake City, the mountain range hedging them in all around. When the elevator door opened to her floor and she stepped across the threshold, his hand let go of her but his eyes did not. He could not wait until the morning to make sure this dream was real.

Michelle wore a pinstriped blue and white blouse that tied around the waist in the back with navy dress pants and heels the first morning of the trade show. Sitting on a bus heading for the convention center, Lasse was also wearing a blue pinstriped dress shirt and navy trousers. The pair sat together in one bus seat and reviewed the plans for the day. They entered the convention center and as they passed by the glass windows Michelle noted the reflection they created. They were beautiful together. Michelle paused and pointed, whispering to Lasse, "Beautiful couple." He stared intently into her eyes and nodded his agreement without a word.

After the disappointing first day at the trade show they rode the bus back to the Grand America to prepare themselves for meeting with the new master distributor from San Diego. Lasse and Michelle discussed the lack of attendance at the show and the missed opportunities but Michelle said, "The International Fire Chiefs show is in another month and I am sure the attendance there will be notable. This product is meant for the fire service! You guys just need to get it in front of the end users." She was right.

They crossed the crystal chandeliered foyer at the Grand America and headed towards the elevator, passing by a round table with a huge floral arrangement that filled the area with the sweet and clean fragrance of frangipani. A young woman was sitting with a large concert harp and the notes of "All I Ask of You," from The Phantom of the Opera reverberated from the high ceilings. The elevator doors opened and the occupants vacated, while Lasse held the doors open for Michelle to enter. She was still talking when the doors closed and Lasse seized her in his arms and for the first time he kissed her, pouring all of his desire for her into one long, fiery kiss. Fused were lips, tongues, breaths, and souls. Michelle returned his kiss fiercely until she melted in his arms. "Oh my word," she gasped when the doors opened to her floor.

"I will meet you in the foyer at 6:30, Ma'am," Lasse breathed, his face almost touching hers; then he let her go.

That was the kiss that ended all other possibilities of any other paths on their lives' journeys. He was it for her and she was it for him. That was the kiss they would tell of to every person they forever met in the future, from North America, Central America, Europe, Australia – they told their story a thousand times or maybe ten thousand. Each time the retelling was like experiencing that first kiss over and over, falling in love with each other and living in that moment repeatedly. Many years later Lasse ordered Michelle to write this story; he didn't want it forgotten. The love of these two people and that first kiss has been relayed and will forever travel into eternity as the beginning of their own personal scripture.

The events of the evening and the dinner meeting with their coworkers were a blur until Lasse asked Michelle, "Ma'am, do you think that later tonight I could come to your room?"

Michelle looked at this beautiful man who had stolen her very soul with just that one kiss and replied with raised eyebrows and a stern tone, "Yes, but nothing will happen but talking, got it?"

"Got it," he grinned.

As they sat on the elegant Richelieu sofa in Michelle's suite, Lasse continued with telling more of the story of his life. He pulled her across his lap so that his breath mingled with hers as he talked with her face to face, looking deeply through her eyes and into her soul. He wanted her to know him better than anyone else, to understand him, and he could see she hung on his every word because she did truly want to know him. He kept one arm around her waist and with the other they held hands as he poured out his heart to her. She felt safe in his arms and knew that it was okay to be vulnerable with him. His voice was so soothing to her that she laid her head on his chest feeling the rapid beat of his heart. Her eyes closed as she continued asking him questions, smiling and storing his answers in her heart. She loved every word of the story of his life. Nothing, not the past loves he had, nothing took away from the story he would write with her; it was all part of him, this man she loved. And she did love him with all of her being and she would for the rest of existence. She wondered if somehow she always had loved him. She could feel the forlorn little boy's experiences as if they were her own. To Michelle, Lasse's story was like remembering from a long time ago.

Lasse bent his head towards Michelle and began to kiss her, their souls further inflamed from the intimate connection. The next few hours of time were spent consumed with fierce, passionate kisses but the woman had a resolve of steel and the man respected that. Lasse wore Chanel's Egoiste cologne and at first Michelle found it unpleasant but that particular scent on Lasse's skin mixed with her own vanilla perfume created a sensual fragrance that would awaken her olfactory receptors and trigger the memory of these moments for the rest of her life. He devoured her with his mouth; and ignited, she fueled his passion responding with the same fervor. She could smell his cologne on her skin as she slept alone in her room that night. She was still smiling.

That August in Salt Lake City was the beginning of a completely different life for both Lasse and Michelle. It would take time, years in fact, to look back and see the course corrections in their lives that caused them to collide and to become one. Lasse was the only man Michelle had ever respected and trusted. She gave her heart to him completely. Lasse's soul was resurrected from a lonely life that had left him emotionally out of tune to one that played like Smetana's symphonic poem, "The Moldau". He had found his home in her.

# CHAPTER SIX

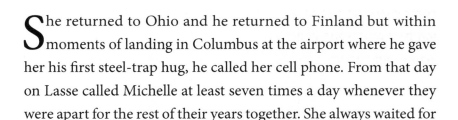

She returned to Ohio and he returned to Finland but within moments of landing in Columbus at the airport where he gave her his first steel-trap hug, he called her cell phone. From that day on Lasse called Michelle at least seven times a day whenever they were apart for the rest of their years together. She always waited for his calls with great anticipation and he always called.

"So, do you see yourself becoming my mistress?" he asked from his home office phone in Masala, Finland.

"Uh, no. No way," Michelle replied resolutely. Hell, no, she would not be anyone's mistress!

"I didn't think so but I had to ask."

"Why would you ask something like that?"

Lasse moved forward with his premeditated conversation and said, "So, you are going to require that I marry you?"

"Is that a proposal?" What the hell kind of proposal is this, she wondered. Is this a proposal?!

"Not officially, but I want to be clear where we stand with each other."

The emails exchanged were full of stories of their pasts and pictures of each other, which at that time took forever to load on home computers with dial up internet. Michelle waited impatiently as one particular photo of Lasse came through that was nothing less than sensual. He was sitting at his desk at his home in Masala wearing Levis, a navy blue polo shirt, Timberland boots, his left ankle hiked across his right knee, lips parted ever so slightly, and a direct gaze that said he wanted her. She was completely enamored with Lasse and fully dedicated to him. He titled that photo, "As You See Not Possible," indicating that the chair he was sitting in would not be efficient for amorous activities. Michelle cracked up and absolutely loved that photo. She put it in a frame and always kept it in plain sight to keep her lover ever before her.

One story he wrote in an email described a very irate husband chasing him when he was yet a teenager. Lasse wrote the words, "He chased me with a knife and he stubbed me." What? Stubbed? Stubbed his what? Oh my gosh, she had already promised to marry the man and he just said he was stubbed. Was this a Finnish way of saying someone had cut his penis off? Michelle paced the floor wondering just how short stubbed could be. What did this mean for their future intimate life? Had he fathered three children after being stubbed? Was that even possible?

Lasse's call came a few hours later, 10pm Finnish time. Michelle broached the subject boldly. "Lasse, you said in your email that the angry husband attacked you with a knife and stubbed you; what does this mean?"

"What?!" he chortled loudly. "No! He stabbed me!"

"Oh, thank the Lord! I thought you meant he cut your penis off!"

"No! There is nothing wrong with my penis!"

"Good because you never know if we may want to have children of our own someday. Oh my word, I have been in horrific worry all afternoon."

Lasse moved on with the conversation but Michelle continued to get the giggles all throughout their discussions that evening. She was so relieved, so happily relieved.

Another afternoon phone call did reveal that Lasse had received the worrisome news that his PSA level showed that he most likely had prostate cancer. Again, before anything more intimate than kisses had transpired between them, the extreme level of commitment between their souls was like the foundation of that ancient stone fortress.

"I do not know what this will mean," Lasse explained. "I do not know if I will die from this or how long I will live."

"Lasse, no matter what, I will take care of you," Michelle promised with all her heart, tears filling her eyes. He knew that he had found someone who didn't want anything more from him than just himself. He knew that Michelle honestly loved him and she would keep her word to take care of him. No one had ever taken care of him. He was the one who always took care of everyone else in his life, fulfilled their wishes, met their needs and God had blessed him with this one person who would stand by him regardless of the dark valley and walk through with him, holding hands with fingers interlocked. She would face and battle all the demons that set out to destroy him. He could let his guard down, be vulnerable, and he knew she would have his back. She was the answer to his prayers. He needed her more than either of them understood and he thanked God for her.

Michelle imagined right then what it would mean if Lasse had to endure chemotherapy treatments or radiation; loss of hair, loss of vitality, horrific vomiting and diarrhea, loss of the love of her life, separation from her own soul. He became her most precious treasure. There was nothing she wouldn't do to save his life. She vowed to live a full life with Lasse and to make every one of his dreams come true. After God, Lasse was most important in her life; she loved him more than she loved herself. Many people would not understand why she chose to serve him as she did; but she made a promise and she kept her word. He was her king and she would always be his queen.

Lasse arrived in Cincinnati for a long date weekend with Michelle in late November. International flights and a seven hour time difference couldn't deplete the excitement he felt to be able to spend this time with her; in fact, his energy was at a high when he saw her waiting for him at the luggage carousel. She was wearing a crisp, white blouse tucked into a black plaid calf-length skirt and black boots. There she was blonde, voluptuous, and smiling radiantly with genuine anticipation. He rushed to her and swooped her up; laughing, he kissed her deeply in front of God and everyone in that airport. Michelle was exhilarated by Lasse's kisses. Their passion for one another was insuppressible and it was an hour before they had pulled out of the airport parking garage.

The first weekend they spent together was at a Marriott in Sharonville, Ohio. Sleep deprived and physically exhausted from the sheer joy of consummating their relationship they both drifted off to sleep as the sun began to rise. Not long afterwards Michelle was awakened by Lasse chuckling in his sleep. He was dreaming and laughing.

"Lasse, what's the matter?" she asked him.

"Nothing at all, I am just so happy," he smilingly murmured in a huskier accent than usual. "And I need a cigarette and some coffee, Ma'am," he stated as he whacked her buttocks. "Wake up!" he ordered. She giggled and scrambled across the bed, heading for the bathroom.

They dressed and breathed deeply of the brisk, late November air. Lasse's hand encompassed Michelle's to keep her hand warm while walking to a nearby shop for coffee and ingredients needed for sandwiches. She asked him to teach her some Finnish words but her attempts of the tongue twister language only brought loud guffaws. Once they returned to their room they were hungry for more of each other rather than the food.

Another night spent in rapturous enjoyment and this time when Michelle woke, Lasse was crying in his sleep.

Michelle shook him lightly and whispered, "Lasse, wake up. What is the matter? You are crying."

He pulled her closer, holding her tightly, and whispered, "I love you, Michelle." The way he said her name was unique to him, his accent elongating the letter i into a long e sound. She cherished hearing her name from his lips.

Tears stung her eyes and brokenly she whispered, "I love you, too, Lasse. I love you forever." She ran the tip of her finger down the length of his perfect nose and to his cheek to trace a tear. What an overwhelming sensation to have a man laugh with joy and then cry with deep emotion while in her arms. She would love this man regardless of the trials life was sure to bring. Oh, how she thanked

God for bringing him into her life. Whatever hell life had been it was all worth it just to be with Lasse. Whatever roads needed to be traveled to be at this very latitude, longitude, time, and space was worth every heartache and hurt. Whatever the cost, it was worth it.

Lasse, wearing only his Finnish dog tags, held Michelle tightly to the hard sinews of his body and asked, "Do you love me fiercely, Michelle?"

She smiled and bit his bottom lip, "You know I do, Lasse."

He pierced her soul with his eyes and tenderly placed his dog tags around her neck. Without added words, it was understood; she belonged to him and he belonged to her.

Michelle cried as Lasse walked through the security and onward to his gate at the airport. At the last place that he would be able to see her, he turned and waved, blowing a big kiss to her. She beamed through her tears and pretended to jump up and catch his airborne kiss. Hopefully their loving enthusiasm inspired others because they were simply crazy about each other. Lasse called her when his connecting flight landed in Schiphol Airport and he relayed the most audacious descriptions of his desires for his favorite parts of her body. He most definitely was her pirate and she his noble lady.

In December Michelle flew to Finland to spend the last week of the year with Lasse; he had invited her to be introduced to all of his family. The first two days and nights they met no one but stayed in his home enjoying every inch of each other that they had missed over the last month.

Michelle received a very special gift from Lasse, something so marvelous and unexpected. Lasse had mailed one of her photos to his artist friend in Riyadh and the man had painted her portrait. It was amazing. It was hanging in Lasse's house and dated 25 September

2001. This man was more than incredible to her. The gift she brought to him was less extravagant but she wanted to share a little of her faith and beliefs with him. She gave him the book, "He Still Moves Stones," by Max Lucado, which allowed them to discuss all things spiritual and to gain a better understanding of each other.

Lasse invited his children and their spouses to dinner, which he and Michelle prepared together. It was an elk roast that was piled on top of mashed potatoes, with a kind of mote to hold the gravy, and garnished with Finnish lingonberries. Lasse had hunted and killed the elk himself, relishing the retelling of the event to Michelle; yes, he was bragging but she adored him. Michelle had brought fine white flour from the States and made her award-winning apple pie. Lasse's family was polite and even kind, and all of them raved about her pie. Lasse's first granddaughter, three-month old Vivian, was held and cherished upon sight. That little baby girl would always be a treasure to Michelle. Michelle opened her heart to all of them and hoped they would meld as a family.

Lasse drove Michelle on icy highways to downtown Helsinki to meet his sister, Marjukka. Michelle loved her on sight and hugged her tightly when they first met. Marjukka said, "Thank you so much, dear Michelle, for making my big brother so happy. I knew when I saw your picture and saw those beautiful eyes that you were the one for him."

Lasse could not resist making Michelle squeal with laughter while driving back to his home by doing donuts on the ice. This must be an innate character in all men to frighten women by skidding their cars on ice.

"Lasse Paivola!" Michelle shouted, "Stop that right now!" But he just grinned at her with a crazed look in his eyes and pretended to vocally rev his engine, spinning out some more.

Lasse heated his sauna and took Michelle for an authentic Finnish sauna experience. The only other sauna she'd had was in Montana and she wore her bathing suit for cooling off in the creek then. Although Lasse had seen her nude several times, sitting and sweating was not the same for her. He sat naked and sweated while she sat sweating in a tank top and a pair of his boxers. They showered together sans the tank top and boxers, but to Lasse it was an odd hang up that Michelle had. From then on she always chose to wear a towel to the sauna.

They visited museums and bookstores in downtown Helsinki where the harbors were completely frozen. Lasse kissed Michelle fiercely in every public place they stopped. He promised her that is was perfectly acceptable to share public displays of affection; she just laughed and enjoyed his kisses. He was her entire world and she did not care what others may think. The air was colder than Michelle had ever experienced and she had been born northeast of Cleveland right on Lake Erie. She knew cold. They visited newborn baby granddaughter, Ira, at the hospital on her birthday, December 31st. Here was another precious little one to add to her prayer list and her heart.

Lasse drove Michelle to Somerniemi for New Year's Eve, the home he had bought for his parents. The winding roads led them through forests of the exceptionally hard Finnish pine trees and fields of barren birch trees that nakedly hibernated until the snows would melt in the spring. This little farm was a new place for them to share their love and their souls. Lasse declared his desires and Michelle met all of them, whether on the stairs to the loft, on the kitchen table, or in the sauna. The bed in the loft was sturdy, seemingly made for the voracious love they shared. Every corner of that little home was marked by their love and presence. They loved and laughed and sang and enjoyed each other. Space and time at Somerniemi would always be changed by their happiness in that place.

The winter in Finland is mainly dark because of being partially located in the Arctic Circle. The happiness both Lasse and Michelle felt could not be dimmed just because the sun did not reach the northern climes in late December. This was now a new year and each day in January brought them closer to each other and to brighter days. Their commitment to each other was going to get them through many years and dangerous trials that would include the valley of the shadow of death. But the elation of being together could not be dimmed.

It was time for Michelle to wave goodbye at the last moment to Lasse at the international airport just outside of Helsinki. She turned and blew him a kiss with a great big smile and he pretended to catch it and hold it to his heart. People must have really thought they were crazy in Finland as everyone is mainly quiet and stoic. Michelle turned the corner towards her gate and Lasse hurried towards a door. For whatever reason, God allowed Michelle to catch one last glimpse of Lasse. He was pulling his coat collar up to hide the fact that he was crying. He never knew that she had seen this; she never told anyone but it stayed in her heart that maybe she meant more to Lasse than he was able to say in words. It was always hardest on the one left behind whenever they said goodbye.

No matter what was occurring in either of their work lives, Lasse planned a hot date weekend once a month with Michelle. He flew from Finland to Ohio and back again with a new vitality for life. They began to plan their lives together. Lasse had met Michelle's sons, Michael and Christopher. He appreciated that they were polite and well-mannered, mature and very good kids. They thought he was cooler than Clint Eastwood. Michelle and Lasse had dinner together with her sister, Heather, who was hilarious.

Lasse visited the International School of Helsinki and found out how to get Michael and Christopher enrolled in high school in Finland. The boys were excited about the possibilities of living abroad and Michelle was pleased that Lasse and her sons were forming their own loving relationships.

In March both Lasse and Michelle were attending the same fire service trade show in Indianapolis for their respective companies. She was thoroughly enjoying selling her German-made leather firefighting boots and Lasse was still involved in the battle for getting the Finnish communication systems introduced to the American market. At the end of the first day of the trade show they were both a bit weary but met in Michelle's hotel room where she was staying with her company. She still had a dinner meeting to attend with her coworkers, the German supplier, and some very high profile fire chiefs but she took what time she could with Lasse. Trade shows were exhausting but were required to build relationships with the customers.

Lasse and Michelle stood at the end of the bed in her room, both still wearing their winter coats. Their arms wrapped around each other they fell to the bed and just held one other, laying side by side and looking into each other's eyes and giving tiny kisses to and nibbling on each other's lips. Lasse whispered, "Michelle, do you marry me?"

So, this was the official proposal, asked in his own personal Finnish to English translation. Without hesitating, Michelle answered, "Yes, Lasse, I marry you forever."

"I do not have your ring yet but it is being made especially for you. I will bring it with me the next time. Is that okay?"

Okay? He didn't have to give her a ring. He had given her his heart and that is all she would ever want. But, yeah, that was okay, it was more than okay. Really? He was having a ring made for her? Lasse Paivola and all his surprises, too? She was more blessed than she could have ever asked and she thanked God every day for this man. She loved him more than she loved her own being.

April came and Lasse brought with him a beautiful emerald cut sapphire ring set all around by diamonds that sparkled like stars in the night sky. He told her to choose the best restaurant in Cincinnati for their special evening. They dined at The Celestial with some of the greatest panoramic views of the city. Lasse wore a suit and tie and Michelle wore the same black suit from the day more than a year earlier when her life was forever altered as Lasse said, "You're freezing, let's go."

When they had finished their dinners of petite filet mignon, Lasse produced a small red box with the ring. He opened it slowly, hoping Michelle would love it. It was an oddity about Michelle that jewelry and gifts never meant so much to her but she loved the ring. To her the sapphire served as a reminder of the sacredness of the relationship with her lover.

"Lasse, it is beautiful," she breathed. He slid the ring on her finger. This dazzling, sweet girl was going to be his wife. In Europe sapphire rings were typically given to royalty and symbolized faithfulness, holiness, wisdom, and virtue. Lasse chose this royal blue sapphire over the standard American diamond solitaire as an intended exception, as Michelle was to him.

# CHAPTER SEVEN

During the following months they designed plans for their new life together. The San Diego master distributor of the communication products decided not to renew his contract after the first year was completed so Lasse would move to the United States with Michelle and the boys. This time Michelle did convince Lasse that together they could sell this product to the American fire service market. Her faith was so strong that Lasse believed her. Again, she was right.

Lasse sold his house in Masala, Finland, packed his belongings into crates that would be shipped across the Atlantic by cargo container, and once again left his homeland in October of 2002.

Michelle sold her five acre hobby farm and began looking for homes in Brookville so the boys could maintain their education in the same school district. She took her boys to see a few possible homes that she and Lasse were considering through email and one huge ugly house stood out. It looked like the Salt Lake City and County Building where Lasse and Michelle had shared the sweetest days more than a year earlier, but it lacked the character and sand-stone carvings. It was a newly built home, unfinished, and abandoned by the owner.

Michael, being artistic, loved it and said, "Mom, if this house is still for sale when Lasse moves here, it is going to be ours."

Michelle firmly replied, "Michael, this house is so ugly we will never even look at it."

Incredibly that very house became their family home. With five bedrooms, four bathrooms, an unfinished basement that would become the office of ProComm Americas, and 4,000 square feet it was perfect for them. The life they lived in that home was truly happy.

Lasse and Michelle married October 12, 2002 in the Brookville City Office. Lasse wore a navy suit with a light blue shirt and a pais-ley tie of blue, red, and pink while Michelle wore the pale pink suit from the first day she shook hands with Lasse when he criticized her driving. Michelle told Lasse that a church wedding would be neces-sary for her to feel truly married before God and he agreed to that.

Every evening they would have dinner together in their dining room. Sometimes Michael and Christopher's friends would sit around the table after dinner, all the boys listening intently to Lasse's sailor stories and dangerous adventures in the Middle East. Those same friends would tease Lasse and call him "Osama bin Lasse" or "Lasse bin Laden"; they all loved him and Michael and Christopher were so proud of him. He became the dad they needed and he completed their family entirely.

Lasse was there to help them prepare for their proms and getting them into their tuxedos, instructing them to keep their jack-ets on and to dance with the ugly girls, too. Lasse was the only one at home while Michelle went to take pictures of the boys when the doorbell rang and there stood Eric, Christopher's friend, in need of a dad to help him with his tie. Lasse was the dad shouting in the football stands to the Brookville Blue Devils, "Nail the fucking idiots!" before Michelle had to quickly escort him to the smoking section away from the delicate crowd. This wasn't a Finnish hockey game and some Americans in that small town were quite gentle. He was the dad who ordered Christopher to take Michael inside while he took a hammer to Michael's car to fix it. He was the dad who told them that fighting fairly was for weak gentlemen and that if someone attacked them they were to kick them in the balls, stomp on their face, and run like hell.

Lasse taught and instructed both boys how to measure, cut, stain, and put up crown molding and baseboards with shoe boards in their new home. He worked hour after hour, day and night to make that home a castle fit for his queen. There was lighting to be selected indoors and out, interior doors, and kitchen appliances, and carpet for the three bedrooms on the third floor. Michelle studied and selected curtains, wood flooring for the main floor, kitchen cabinet styles, and faucets for every sink. Lasse built the office in the basement with bookshelves and extra windows for plenty of light. The basement had an abundance of space for a pool table and a bar, as well as a library and a custom made Finnish sauna with shower and large dressing room that Lasse designed himself.

All of the Finnish family came to visit them during the summers and there was plenty of room for them to stay for weeks. Marianne and her family, Jere and his family, and Lauri and his wife would all come for visits. Lasse's sister, Marjukka, visited twice, and his cousin, Ismo, came to stay for a week as well.

Every night Lasse and Michelle went to the sauna then sipped tea on their deck, studying the stars and talking about everything between heaven and earth. Whether winter or summer, they watched for passing satellites or shooting stars and swatted mosquitoes and made plans for the twenty five years Lasse promised Michelle. The fifteen years they lived together as a family in their unique castle was the longest that either Lasse or Michelle had ever lived anywhere in their lives. It was home.

# CHAPTER EIGHT

·•·❧·•·

That blonde haired little girl with the sea green eyes who had been left at an orphanage by her family in 1973 was married to her Prince Charming in an 11th century church in Hameenlinna, Finland and had the most amazing reception in the wine cellar of a castle on April 10, 2004.

Michelle tackled making the wedding arrangements through phone calls and emails. Her sister, Heather, went wedding dress shopping with her and insisted on the veil that twinkled with Swarovski crystals. Michelle felt like a princess and decided, what the heck? She was going for it! On her drive home from the Northern Kentucky bridal shop she heard for the first time on the radio the Christian song by Mercy Me, "I Can Only Imagine." She sang to Jesus with all her heart and thanked Him for this most amazing life story and she could imagine standing before the Lord with a grateful heart.

All of their family gathered in Hameenlinna, Finland for their marriage dedication. Michael and Christopher flew to Finland with Lasse and Michelle. Michelle's sister, Heather, and her husband,

Mike, traveled to Finland with Samantha, who was just six years old, and little Gus, who was only four. Lasse and Mike had become as close as brothers or maybe as a father and son during their years of hunting in Kentucky. Lasse was pleased to have him at the wedding. They stayed at the castle where their reception would be held. Lasse took them all to meet his Uncle Eero and his wife, Marjatta, and then to meet his cousin, Ismo and his wife, Tuula. Uncle Eero and Michelle bonded immediately and he became one of her most cherished family members and she became like a daughter to him.

The night before their ceremony Lasse woke around 3am and said, "It is snowing." Sure enough, when they got up in the morning, it had snowed. Michelle was not worried in the least that this special day would be hampered by a little snow. She loved snow and the added brilliance of the billions of sparkling diamonds covering the ground was something she was grateful for.

The morning began with breakfast in the castle's restaurant. It was very quiet even though there were several guests enjoying their meals. Finns are quiet where Americans are loud. Lasse, Michael, Christopher, and Michelle had all kinds of typical Finnish food to eat; the boys were excited to try anything Finnish. Later, Heather and her family joined them in the dining room. Lasse and Michelle helped them try to find things for the kids to eat, although only Gus managed. Samantha nibbled on a piece of cheese. At that time it was tough for Americans to replace all the sugary and deep fried foods while in Finland. Lasse and Michelle just laughed at their disappointment, even when Heather later declared, "Thank God, a McDonald's; decent food!"

After breakfast Michelle went back to their room and began ironing everyone's outfits. Lasse took Mike and Michael into town to pick up the flowers and to get some food for Heather's family. Michael had to learn to drive in Hameenlinna so that he would be able to take Heather's family back and forth to the church. Christopher stayed with Michelle because he had an upset stomach. It gave them time to chat and have fun together.

While Mike was searching for frozen pizzas, Lasse bought some special car wax to help remove the scratches Michelle had put into the driver's side of their rental car when she backed into a light post at the castle. The wax worked like a miracle and the damage was so minimal that it went unnoticed. She was rather excited and was not paying close attention while backing the car; Lasse wasn't angry but he was grateful to be able to buff the scratches away.

The magical day seemed to pass quickly. Lasse and Michael returned with the flowers and then left again with Christopher to check out a hunting supply store with Mike and Gus. Michelle took a 30-minute nap and then a long bubble bath. She was totally relaxed and not anxious at all. She had time to pray and really thank God for the wonderful blessing of her family and this fairytale day. "Heavenly Father," she gave a half sob, "thank You. You have blessed me beyond my imagination and I don't know why. This life is so incredible. Thank You."

Once Lasse and the boys returned, he took a short power nap and rested himself. Suddenly they realized it was later than they thought and Lasse and Michelle hurried to the wine cellar with their gifts for everyone. They had insisted that no one bring gifts for them but rather they gave gifts to each family member and friend who was there. They finished the gift cards with personal messages, set them out on the tables, deciding who would sit where. They had one Finnish speaking table and one English speaking table. It was their desire that those who only spoke Finnish or English would be comfortable where they were seated.

When they realized it was 4:15, Lasse and Michelle literally ran back to their room. He was pulling her along as quickly as possible and she was giggling with excitement the whole time. They weren't dressed, her hair wasn't fixed and they were supposed to be at the church at 4:30. Michelle could not keep from laughing while she hurried with her makeup. Lasse jumped into the shower and then into his tux.

Heather's family was ready and waiting outside in the corridor between their rooms. Michael and Christopher had readied themselves and looked like handsome grown men in their suits. Michelle gave sweet, little Samantha her old pearl necklace and Christopher helped the beaming princess to put it on. She was wearing an iridescent ice blue full length gown with tiny white gloves and she felt like royalty.

Things moved so quickly. Lasse helped Michelle to put on her dress and she threw on her veil and tiara. Michael held the back of her dress and, still laughing, she was pushed into the car and away they went to the church while she tried desperately to do something with her hair.

When they arrived at Vanajan Kirkko, the church, everyone was already there. It was 4:45! The boys helped Michelle get into the priest's meeting room; Michael was holding the back of her dress and Christopher was holding her. When Michael slipped on the ice and almost fell, they were all laughing. It was a chilly afternoon because of the snowfall, but Uncle Eero had promised sunshine and they were blessed with a radiant day. Everyone was genuinely joyful and the atmosphere was filled with laughter.

Lasse came in to the priest's room where Michelle waited. They were both giddy as they spoke with the priest about being nervous even though they were already married. Lasse looked more handsome than ever. His tux had long tails and his vest was scarlet brocade. His boutonniere of a mini scarlet calla lily matched Michelle's bouquet of scarlet calla lilies, chosen especially for their meaning of passionate devotion. Her thigh-highs began to slip past her knees and she begged Lasse to remove them. Right in front of the priest, he got down on his knees, crawled under Michelle's dress, and removed her hose. They both laughed infectiously and the priest found them endearing. They could not have been happier.

The caretaker took them around to the front of the church and they waited in between the double doors of the ancient building while the music began. They were both nervous but Lasse gave Michelle a great kiss and she calmed down. Her insides were quivering with excitement and joy. The caretaker opened the doors and down the aisle they went. They were talking to each other the entire time while cameras flashed and they were smiling at all of their loved ones. These moments were cherished and incredible to both of them.

At the altar the priest, Pappi Juha, chuckled at them as he waited in front of the ryijy, the special wedding carpet Finns have used for centuries as a prayer rug. They held hands and both knelt on the ryijy and Pappi Juha prayed over them. They stood again and he began to relay the story of how they met, Lasse fired Michelle, she hated him, and eventually they came to love each other. He shared how their interests all revolved around food and Michelle started to get the giggles. It just seemed hilarious that all of their mutual interests entailed food, being "fat Americans". Michelle ordered herself to calm down and Lasse squeezed her hand. The priest then asked

Lasse if he promised to love, honor, and be faithful in sorrow and in joy, first in English and then in Finnish. Lasse said, "I will; tahdon," answering first in English and then in Finnish.

Then the priest asked Michelle the same and she answered in both English and in Finnish, "I will; tahdon."

Pappi Juha led everyone in the Lord's Prayer and everyone repeated it in their own language. They exchanged their rings and a sweet and proper kiss all the while Ismo was taking pictures. Michael and Christopher read the love verses from 1 Corinthians 13. They had said they were nervous but their voices were both so deep and strong that they didn't sound nervous at all.

Lasse and Michelle simply beamed and headed down the aisle to the back of the church and up into the balcony to wait while all the family went outside. When they joined them it was beautifully sunny and the family threw rice at them, as was the tradition in Finland. Tuula, Ismo's wife, managed a half a cup of rice right in between Michelle's bosom. Later Michelle retrieved it and had Gus hand it back to Tuula, who smiled mischievously. It was just so much fun and recorded as one of the best days of their lives.

Michael drove them to the castle for the grand reception. Everyone was already waiting on them and Lasse gave the toast. Whatever he said was in Finnish and at last he said, "…and the same thing in English!"

The food was amazing. The tray of Baltic herring was beautiful, and although Michelle didn't touch it, Lasse devoured it. She had the tar salmon and it was so perfectly prepared it melted in her mouth. There was also liver pate and a tender roast lamb. They had Vorschmack, a Finnish dish of chopped herring filets, which was interestingly delicious, along with roast beef. They were then served cloudberry parfait that was light, slightly tart, and a tiny bit sweet.

Lasse and Michelle were up and speaking with all their guests. She took a photo album she had created with pictures of each person present over to the Finnish table and let them look through it. She wanted them all to know how cherished they were. Family is the truest and dearest treasure.

They opened the gifts Lasse and Michelle had brought them, but it was so dark in the wine cellar that they could barely see what they were. The entire celebration was so much fun. Finally, they brought in the cake and Pappi Juha whispered to Michelle that the tradition was that the first to step on the other's toes after cutting the cake would be the boss of the family. She stepped on Lasse's toes immediately to tease him with this tradition. The cake was delicious. Marjukka said, "This cake is just like the one our mother used to make for special occasions!" Those kind words blessed Michelle's soul. Lasse often spoke so tenderly of his mother and Michelle wished she could have met the woman who had brought this man she loved with all her being into life. Little tidbits like the comment of their cake were treasured by her.

Lasse started to wrap things up for the evening because he knew the little granddaughters were tired and needed to get home. Michelle still hadn't told him about the surprise she had arranged; a big fireworks production. So, she tried to hurry the fireworks demonstrator but he couldn't really change the schedule because things were already timed and planned. Michelle had to tell Lasse that they had one more surprise for everyone and he insisted on knowing what it was.

Everyone put on their coats and headed to the terrace. They waited in the dark until the incredible show began. It was so amazing! There was another wedding party going on in the castle and they joined Lasse and Michelle's party on the terrace, including all the members of their band. Even the castle staff was out on the terrace. It was just beautiful and Michelle was beaming. She wasn't watching the fireworks; she was watching the excitement on everyone else's faces. Fireworks demonstrations are very rare in Finland so this was a grand surprise.

They all kissed goodbye and said it was the best wedding and reception they'd ever been to. When Lasse's daughter-in-law, Hanna, hugged Michelle she said the most memorable sentiment, "You look like an angel!" Michelle stole those endearing words and repeated them to the brides at every wedding she attended from then on. What a treasure, the most amazing love for each other and family. This was an incredible fairytale written by God's own hand.

# CHAPTER NINE

—⊷⊗⊶—

Michelle tried valiantly to learn the very difficult Finnish language. She made a few major mistakes quite publically and Lasse ordered her to never use Finnish again. Every summer Lasse and Michelle traveled to Finland for business meetings and to visit all the family there. They always hosted a family dinner at Somerniemi, Lasse's little farm. One June they planned an American cookout for the Finnish family. Lasse grilled hotdogs and hamburgers, and buns were brought from America. Michelle made her homemade apple pie, baked beans, potato salad, and deviled eggs. There were inquiries made as to what "deviled eggs" were and as Michelle carefully contemplated her answer, she chose the word she had learned for devil and the word she had learned for eggs. The end result, said before the entire family, grandchildren and babies alike, was "Satan's mother-fucking testicles".

Gentle, proper Jere sat rigidly and kindly said in a grave tone, "Michelle…..we don't say words like that in front of the children." What in the world had she said? Deviled eggs. Lasse fumed as the entire family looked at him, knowing there was only one source Michelle could have learned those words. She was innocent and he was guilty. He was so pissed off and embarrassed that he ordered her to never speak Finnish again.

Their lives together were not without struggles, shouting, and slammed doors; they were both passionate people, but healing always took place in one another's arms. He could still be a pompous ass and she was difficult, complicated, stubborn, and as ridiculously infuriating as ever. But it worked. They were made for each other. They fought with each other and fought against the world together. And everyone loved and adored them. In each fire department, police station, and military base they were asked how they met. The story always began with, "In Finland you would get a ticket for that." Michelle would reenact her expression while mockingly repeating Lasse's first words to her. Lasse would follow with the fact that he had fired her and then he would say, "I thought she married me for love; but, no, it was for revenge!" Everyone always laughed and admired the happy, beautiful couple. This happened everywhere they went.

Everyday life was full of rigorous, creative fun and adventure; this included their love life. Even after a few years of marriage they managed to daily delight themselves with one another. Together they vibrated at a rare frequency and Michelle was certain that they had even invented some escapades. Lasse made a trip to Finland each year without Michelle but made up for each day gone within the first twenty-four hours of his return. Once she surprised him at the airport wearing nothing but her mink coat and high heels. They didn't leave the airport parking garage until an hour later but both were happily satisfied.

The first years were not without the prostate cancer worries; however, after thorough research they were assured that "watchful waiting" would be enough for the time being. They seriously discussed having a child together and there were pregnancy tests at times but they were always negative. When Lasse's PSA level, the prostate-specific antigen determining malignancy, started to rise they had already researched hospitals from Johns Hopkins to Loma Linda and Mayo Clinic and MD Anderson, east coast to west coast and Minnesota to Texas but one of the top Cleveland hospitals was most experienced with the type of treatment Lasse wanted. Brachytherapy would not cause incontinence or impotence, both which would have been intolerable for Lasse. Lasse and Michelle were very open and honest about their physical relationship with Lasse's oncologist, Dr. John Smith; who was the most compassionate and competent doctor they had met. He understood and he supported their decision, he advised, and he befriended them. For years following his careful surgical placement of the radioactive seeds into Lasse's prostate, they would travel all the way to Cleveland for doctor visits that could have been managed in Dayton, just to see Dr. Smith.

During the year following the brachytherapy there were many blood tests to make sure the PSA levels were coming down instead of climbing. Fear of losing Lasse gripped Michelle and became more than she could handle. For months she had shortness of breath and a constant choking feeling, she was visiting doctors herself to determine the problem. It was fear that was choking her. Lasse took her to Martha's Vineyard for a week and with a lot of prayer and understanding that these things were out of her control, her anxiety subsided. She changed her diet and ate mainly fruits and vegetables;

she also tried to get more sleep and she drank less coffee. But it was finally putting Lasse's health, which she could not control, into the hands of God that brought her peace.

# CHAPTER TEN

L asse and Michelle started their company, ProComm Americas, in November 2002. The first years following 9/11 the U.S. government allotted multi-millions of dollars for safer communication. This created an open door for ProComm Americas and the Finnish-made communication system. Lasse and Michelle traveled all over the States training dealers in their product line and they were welcomed into fire departments, police departments, and on to military bases. The sales came slowly and in the beginning not at all. Michelle told Lasse that she was going to pray and ask the Lord to send some orders. He said that was wrong, that God intended for them to work harder. She prayed anyway. Less than five minutes after she prayed, the fax machine churned out an order from an unknown customer: the Godly, Texas Fire Department had ordered two units. Michelle chuckled; very funny, God. And the fax machine cranked out another order, and another, and another until by the end of the day Lasse ordered Michelle, "Tell Him to turn it off now, we can't handle all these orders!" They were completely grateful and felt so blessed.

Being a former diplomat, Lasse had a certain set of skills that most people do not even understand how to acquire or even recognize when they are being used on them. There came a time when the Finnish supplier, the very company where Lasse had been the Managing Director when he first met Michelle, began manufacturing in China. Their high-end communication system immediately lost its quality and the real battles began. Lasse had to travel to many major fire stations and help solve the technical issues. Sometimes the units wouldn't transmit, or they would cease to work altogether, some sizzled, and once in a city-wide meeting Lasse said the units actually smoked. Lasse's certain set of skills and his years of forcing the sale of goods in marine underwriting, allowed ProComm Americas to retain their great customer service reputation while the Finnish supplier did not. Lasse entered a meeting with a major city fire department who was ready to sue the Finnish supplier for all of the $125,000 they had spent on their non-working equipment. Lasse listened intently to all their complaints, their worries for safety, and the potential for lost lives. His heart was to provide safe communication and never risk anyone's life for any amount of money. He became a kind of hero to the heroes. They knew he would go to the supplier and kick their balls to make the situation right. And that is just what he did. As he left that meeting, he had a purchase order from them for more units in his hand. Yes, he certainly did. That situation went from a probable law suit to their faith in him resulting in them asking for more. He was dedicated and they trusted him. Lasse and Michelle built this same kind of trusting relationship all over the country.

In one fire department in North Carolina the Finnish product failed embarrassingly. They traveled there multiple times and Lasse had all of the equipment shipped back to Finland to be rebuilt. It wasn't just wrongly printed circuit boards but faulty components and it could have cost lives. Lasse and Michelle flew to Finland where if ever there was a time Lasse growled dissatisfaction it was then. He threatened and warned that the Finnish company was going to kill somebody if they didn't get the products made properly. Honestly, the Finns who were running the company at that time didn't seem the least bit bothered by the warnings but they did agree to rebuild the units for the department in North Carolina. Lasse and Michelle met with that department once the reworked units arrived and the supplier had sent one of their Finnish engineers along. As they pulled each unit of the three hundred and fifty out of their boxes to test them, components came apart in their hands. The female Nexus plug would come right out when the male was unplugged. Both Lasse and Michelle were deeply worried and humiliated. Their Finnish engineer set up a soldering and testing station on the spot. One of the battalion chiefs looked at everyone in the room, the dealer who had sold the units, the Finnish engineer, as well as at Lasse. He said in a commanding tone while pointing to Lasse, "He's the only one I trust." Me, too, Michelle thought and she loved and respected Lasse all the more.

A manly lady firefighter strutted into the room, a slight bounce to her boxy frame. She watched silently for a while as the tension in the room kept building while all three hundred and fifty units were tested and half of them failed inspection. Surely she had the sweetest intent of shattering the stress when she looked smolderingly into Lasse's eyes and she said huskily, "You sexy....and you know it, too."

Michelle cracked up and Lasse produced a blush but everyone was so grateful for that lady's comic relief. It was a battle that literally took years but Lasse made sure those units were safe and in good working order for their fire department.

The years passed with Michael graduating high school and attending college, and then Christopher did the same. Christopher married his girlfriend, Marah, at 19 years old and Michael insisted on staying a bachelor and having fun. Lauri married and Lasse said Michael was his one last hope of a young man in their family retaining his freedom. Michelle swatted Lasse's backside and then gave his buttocks a squeeze for his trouble. All their children were grown and the grandbabies kept arriving. Their lives were happy and blessed.

Michelle had spent years in a long distance relationship with God. She was eternally grateful for her life and could not begin to count her many blessings but still she had kept God at arm's length. A phone call from Michael was a turning point.

"Mom," he said as she drove back from a trade show in Indianapolis, "Mike beat Vicki to death." Vicki was Brittany's mother, Michael's former girlfriend. Michelle had personally known Vicki since they were children and had gone to school together.

"What?! Oh my gosh, Michael! Is she okay?"

"Mom – she's dead."

Michelle pulled the car over and Lasse took over driving. What became a nightmare and then great healing for Brittany also began a return of Michelle's spiritual walk with God. She began reading her Bible every morning just trying to make sense of this loss. She poured out her heart to God and felt a renewal in her spirt of being one with her Creator. She called the first hour of her day, "coffee with the Lord" and no matter how early she had to get up or where she was on the planet, He came first. And although she never blamed God for all the bad things that happened in this life, she did trust that He would keep His word to work all things out for good no matter what.

In 2010 Lasse and Michelle had a serious scare with his heart. He had 99% blockage in one of his arteries and they ended up in the local emergency room. The cardiologist on call that night insisted that he would place a stent in Lasse's heart the next day. Michelle said there was no way that was going to happen in that filthy hospital where there was feces on the floor and the cardiologist didn't bother to cover his ratty sweater with his white coat. She contacted Dr. John Smith and asked his recommendation at his hospital in Cleveland. With Dr. Smith's backing, Lasse was able to get in to see Dr. Robert Johnson within two days. He was one of the country's top cardiologists. The stent placement was not without a life-threatening disaster. Michelle waited nervously while the procedure took place. She saw many patients called to the desk and their surgeon would come out and assure the family that their patient was well. When Michelle's name was called they told her to go to a private waiting room. She paced and prayed and waited until Dr. Johnson came into the room. He said nothing but took her in his arms. Michelle was outraged.

"Is he alive? Is he okay?" she demanded. If he said that Lasse had died, she was going to force him to go back in there and make him alive.

"He did just fine," Dr. Johnson assured. Oh, Michelle was so angry at this man, respected and required as he was, getting a hug out of a big-boobed blonde while she was frantic over her husband's life. Michelle rushed to Lasse and stayed by his hospital bedside, sleeping in a chair to watch over him.

Michelle and Lasse were in their car leaving the parking garage of the hospital for a three and a half hour drive back home. As Michelle pulled onto the street from the garage, Lasse said, "Baby, we ain't going home just yet. There is something the size of my fist growing in my pants pocket." The tag that the surgeon had used to close Lasse's femoral artery had torn away and he was bleeding internally.

Immediately Michelle drove right up to the front door of the hospital and got Lasse into a wheelchair and back to Dr. Johnson's office. The younger surgeon, who had performed the stent placement procedure under Dr. Johnson's supervision, was shocked but still able to function. He asked for a crash cart but the physician's assistant was new to that department and couldn't find it. Michelle was in a sobbing panic but Lasse, white as a sheet, remained calm, all the while his fist-sized bulge grew with blood to the size of half a football. Dr. Johnson calmly entered the room, he had a nurse lead Michelle to another patient room, and he lifted Lasse's legs, creating a natural tourniquet. As Lasse was taken back to surgery to install two tags into his femoral artery, Dr. Johnson entered the room where Michelle was waiting and crying. The old doctor had some nerve. He put his arms around her and kissed the top of her head. This made Michelle so angry.

"Is he going to be okay?" she demanded, pulling away from Dr. Johnson. What in the world? She was livid.

Lasse was fine and back home in two days. The blood that had pooled into his groin dissipated over the next few months. During those couple of months Lasse took life very easily. He had to make sure his heart was in good working order. He had promised Michelle twenty-five years. He sat sweetly as she read him an online book, "High Heels to Tractor Wheels" by Ree Drummond, when her blog,

"The Pioneer Woman" was rather new. They laughed together, held hands, kissed, and prayed, so grateful for more time together. Lasse took to baking homemade cinnamon rolls for whatever reason and Michelle loved him all the more.

While Lasse recuperated, Michelle continued working sales appointments and trade shows for ProComm Americas. Lasse took a break from all the travel and Marah, Christopher's wife, began working full time with Michelle. Lasse was a favorite with the Las Vegas Police Department and had even created specialized communication equipment for the SWAT team. He told Marah if she traveled for him with Michelle to Las Vegas, he would make sure she had a great steak dinner while she was there. By the time Marah and Michelle had arrived, spent hours with the SWAT team who gave them the grand tour of every one of their special operations vehicles and flexed all their muscles for the two pretty blondes, the restaurants in their hotel were closed. But they were staying at Bellagio, so who could really complain?

Lasse continued working in ProComm Americas but as the economy in the States had taken a bad turn, many police and fire departments lost their funding for new communication equipment. This meant retaining customers by handling all their repairs so they would keep using their products. Lasse worked days and nights with the repairs as the sales of new equipment declined. The Finnish supplier had withdrawn their promise to contribute to magazine ads and trade show support. ProComm Americas could not sustain the advertising, trade shows, and all the travel with the decline in sales. Lasse was tired of all the repairs. He found satisfaction in creating solutions and new products that worked with the Finnish equipment but he was tired.

# CHAPTER TWELVE

When Lasse left for sea as a merchant sailor at age fourteen he had a dream that someday when he retired he would sail his own boat wherever he wanted. He built that boat in his mind tens of thousands of nights before drifting off to sleep. Many nights he would speak of his plans to Michelle as she asked sleepy questions, listening to the sound of his voice that always comforted her. He would describe the engine and by the time he had moved on from there, Michelle was sleeping.

As the months turned into years that their company was declining, Lasse became cranky. He wanted to begin his sailing plans and close the company. Michelle did not fully understand exactly what he wanted. If she had, she would have worked harder to get him out to sea sooner. Since the beginning of their relationship she was committed to helping Lasse live his dreams. As more equipment came in for repairs, Lasse became irritated that he had not been able to execute his retirement plans, constantly saying, "My time is short," or "My time is running out." Michelle could see that

Lasse was becoming as a caged lion who is supposed to be running free. He was turning mean and sullen.

Michelle asked Lasse what he wanted and he began to tell her in earnest what kind of boat and where he wanted to travel. She was fully engaged in helping him to find that boat. They traveled to Connecticut to look at a pilot house boat and Michelle began to see the charm in this project. How darling, she thought. But that boat was not the one. Lasse would find boats in Florida, all over the East Coast, and around Lake Erie and have Michelle contact the owners or brokers. Her heart was to make her man happy, as she had vowed from the beginning.

On a hot day in September 2012 Lasse and Michelle drove to Toledo and looked at a 1980 Marine Trader Trawler. Lasse was in love and a brand new man. The boat was in excellent condition for her age. She had only 600 actual hours on her engine, and had sat lonely year after year while the owners used her once in a summer but usually didn't move her from her slip (boat parking spot) at the marina. The test drive and an inspection report proved the final answer and Lasse finally bought his retirement boat.

Lasse and Michelle had a completely different perspective on closing ProComm Americas. He wanted it closed forever and she wanted to find another supplier and keep the customers they had built relationships with for the past dozen years. He felt he would still be wrangled in for repairs and other operations and he just wanted to be free of all of it. Being Mr. Command Man, he told her no, and that she would have to find a new career.

"Wait a minute; do you mean you plan to do all this sailing while I stay here at home? You intend for me to live here without you?" For the next five years this would be one of Michelle's worst heartaches. She poured her heart out to God at how unfair for her husband to leave her weeping on the seashore when she had dedicated all of her own life to fulfilling his life. Unfair or not, Lasse was sailing alone.

During that winter and spring of 2013 Lasse drove from home to the marina on Lake Erie every week to prepare Sixteen Tons. He chose the name, "Sixteen Tons" after the Tennessee Ernie Ford song from 1946, the year of his birth. He loved the lyrics, "You load sixteen tons and what do you get? Another day older and deeper in debt." Michelle swore it gave him some sort of justification for spending all of his retirement income on his new sweetheart. All kinds of repairs were necessary and there were provisions needed for his upcoming journeys. Lasse was planning to cruise his boat on the American Great Loop, going across the Great Lakes, down the Mississippi, out across the Gulf of Mexico, around Florida, up the East Coast through the Intracoastal Waterways, down the Hudson River past the Statue of Liberty, through the Erie Canal, and back to Lake Erie. Later he dreamed of buying a sail boat and crossing the Atlantic Ocean for an even more challenging adventure.

Michelle packed his things, provisioned his boat, threw a bon voyage party with family and friends, and kissed him goodbye in August of 2013. They slept together like magnets in his bunk in his captain's quarters the night before he left and as he held her in his arms he said, "Bambina, I will always come home to you."

"And I will always wait for you," she promised.

Lasse and Michelle had spent nearly every moment of the last dozen years side by side and now they were apart. Michelle cried with a broken heart and Lasse loved every minute of sailing. She helped him set up a blog documenting his adventures and she wrote her own blog called, "My Pirate Husband" documenting her struggles to unclog the drains and fight off buzzing locusts and jump starting the lawn mower and shoveling the snow from their three-cars-wide driveway while he was gone from her. She prepared homemade, organic freezer meals for him even though she cried and prayed for Lasse while she cooked for him. She called him selfish and he agreed. He bought her a snow blower and relished telling that story along with all the others when people asked how they had met.

The same month that Lasse left on Sixteen Tons, Michelle and Marah, her daughter-in-law, created a unique preschool curriculum and opened for business. She kept busy teaching 2 and 3 year olds how to read and how to sing praise songs to God in Hebrew. She helped little ones to tie their shoes and Lasse called her on Skype every evening. She resented his absence and he knew it but he couldn't stay home and cut the grass and wax the car. He loved the freedom and adventure of sailing and he knew Michelle was fully committed to him. He had promised her twenty-five years and he fully intended to sit in the rocker with her later, after all his adventures. He was strong and able and he was sailing. Lasse missed Michelle but the thrill of adventure and the vibration of his 120 horse power Ford Lehman under him made him come alive again. All the years of sitting in the basement office repairing the communication equipment were behind him. He had resented the last couple of years sitting there and was glad to finally be free of the worry and responsibility. He called Michelle seven times a day, sang to her, made her laugh, made her angry, made her cry, and thanked her every evening at dinner time for her delicious homemade freezer meals that she signed with a heart or Bible verse. He was happy and blessed and he knew it. He spent hours talking to God out on the Great Lakes and the rivers. When he looked up at the stars he was no longer on the deck with Michelle in small town America but out on the open water without a light for miles, just talking with God about the almost seven decades he had walked this earth under the Heavenly Father's care. He didn't deserve this great life and he was so grateful.

Lasse planned long weekend getaways with Michelle and they strolled all over Savannah and St. Augustine, hand in hand, fingers interlocked. She was gracious and funny, and she loved being with Lasse but in her heart she still felt resentful for having to live without him. She adored him. She would fly to wherever Lasse was and they walked beaches; Tybee Island was their favorite. They visited historical forts and poked around maritime museums. They sipped coffee in small cafes and she still hung on his every word. He planned an amazing surprise weekend, again in Savannah, Georgia and they stayed at the gorgeous two hundred year old inn, 17Hundred90. They walked River Street and had brunch at a tiny window side table overlooking the Savannah River at Huey's on the River. They went in to all the little shops, discussed anything and everything with the shop owners, and once again told the story of how they met and how Lasse had said to Michelle, "In Finland you would get a ticket for that." They shared how she had hated him and that he thought she married him for love, but no, it was for revenge. They told of his boating adventures and Michelle said it could have been worse than to be replaced by a gal named Sixteen Tons. He found and purchased a Greek style sea captain's hat after trying on dozens of others. He wore that hat proudly while Michelle rolled her sea green eyes at him but smiled at the little boy still inside the retired man.

They slept together like magnets and made up for lost nights together. Lasse's kisses still made Michelle swoon. And yet she did hold it against him that he had stolen so much time from their happy lives for his mistress, Sixteen Tons. Michelle forced Lasse to agree that the time he spent boating would be subtracted from his twenty-five year commitment. She would later say, "You still owe me ten years, plus the five you stole for boating!" And he would smack her rump and completely agree to it. There were long weekends spent on the boat and they behaved as always, like young lovers. Lasse was still madly in love with Michelle's bosom and she only pretended to be offended when he spent more time talking with "the sisters" than to her eye to eye. They sang out their arguments, he singing "Fifteen Miles on the Erie Canal" and she belting out "Country Roads Take Me Home". They trusted each other and he had every intention of making up the time to her.

Lasse completed his Great Loop adventure and was home for three weeks. He cut the grass twice and actually waxed the car, changed the lightbulbs, and bought Michelle that brand new, expensive – and as he always told the story, "red" snow blower. Of course, this bit of information was inserted into their love story and she would say that he bought that snow blower for her birthday, a snow blower! And he would add to the story that she didn't speak to him for two weeks! People everywhere still enjoyed hearing their continuing love story. Each of them was always telling strangers about the other.

After the three weeks back at home Lasse said, "I think I'll turn around and go the other way." He needed to be back on the water to feel really alive and the weather would still be good for sailing if he started out of Lake Erie now.

"Turn around and go the other way, hmph," Michelle replied. "You do remember that our neighbor lady said to me, 'You mean

Lasse doesn't live here with you any more'? That is what everyone is thinking while you're gone for weeks at a time and I am left here without you. Go on and go if you're going then. I've lived here a year without you, I guess I can do it again." Michelle was hurt and angry.

"Bambina, you know I can't sit around here and do nothing but cut the grass. I won't do it," he suddenly declared with an edge in his voice. Lasse could not be forced into anything. He had spent too many years of his early life trying to fit into a mold of someone else's making and he would never do that again.

"Fine. I know it doesn't matter to you what it costs me for you to be gone. I am giving up my life, years of my life, for your boating dreams. I have to live every day without you, eat dinner every night alone, and sleep alone while you're out sailing the seven seas like some pirate! You have left me without a hand to hold, Lasse!" Michelle shouted this last and Lasse had no defense. It was true. He knew he was breaking her heart and that she hated being without him by her side but neither was she ready to retire or to leave their family and go with him. But he could not shrivel up and die in this small town; he couldn't make himself do it, even if it meant hurting Michelle. On some level he knew he was putting himself above her; but it was more of a survival mechanism than loving himself more than he did her. She would forgive him and he would give her many more years sitting in the rocker while she fussed over him. It would be okay. They had many years ahead of them for that, now was not the time to take up the rocking chair.

In late August 2014 Michelle waved from the shores of Lake Erie as her pirate husband once again left for his grand adventures. The dramatic, romantic side of Lasse loved seeing her waving from the shore to him, knowing she would always be waiting for him to come home. She drove home from Lake Erie totally pissed off, hot tears of indignation slowly tracking down her cheeks, but missing him all the same. She prayed for him and about her anger with his selfishness the almost three hour drive home. But her heart resented his adventures; bitterness is just fermented unforgiveness and this tiny seed took root in her soul.

Lasse was more diligent in trips home and making sure his hot date weekends with Michelle somehow made up for their time apart. He had driven two days through an ice storm just to get home to the sauna with her, put on a grey wool suit and cufflinks, and then drove to Cincinnati for a stage production of "Pride and Prejudice". Michelle loved the play but Lasse showed her how different a Viking pirate was from the prim and proper English love story for the rest of that night at the Willis Grave's Bed and Breakfast in Burlington, Kentucky. She always felt rejuvenated after those weekends with him and he knew how to put a smile on her face and a song on her lips. "Oh What a Beautiful Morning" was her tune of choice after every night with him.

If Lasse thought he would die without accomplishing his sailing dreams, Michelle nearly died of a broken heart while living without him. But his passionate kisses and fervent devotion to her body when they were together resurrected her soul every time.

On a longer leg of his voyage Lasse had called Michelle from one of the two phones he kept onboard and said he was anchoring near a lonely island and would call her back within thirty minutes. He didn't call; he had always called in all their years together, he had always called. Michelle called both of his cell phones and tried to contact him by Skype and email; nothing. She cried the entire night wondering if she should call the Coast Guard and imagining all sorts of disasters that could have happened to her love. If anything happened to him she didn't know how she would be able to keep breathing. She wept and worried for the next twelve hours and then Lasse called. He said, "I didn't have service for either of these phones, Bambina, I am fine."

"How dare you, Sir! I have sobbed for the last twelve hours! How would I know if you had a heart attack, fell overboard, were attacked by thieves? I wouldn't and I wouldn't be able to help you!"

Lasse tried to appease her but there was nothing that could help. She shouted some more, "If you don't have service then you just keep cruising down the waterways until you do! I will not be made to worry like this, Lasse!"

The time away from each other was hard on both of them. Lasse was lonely, too. He had met many nice retired people that is the yacht cruising community but he missed that noble lady back at home. He had her homemade freezer meals every day and he kissed her goodnight over the phone each night but he missed her touch. He needed her strength and assurance. He hadn't told her but he was having signs of some more serious bowel issues and the problems weren't clearing up even after a few months. He needed her hand to hold. She was still ridiculously infuriating but he loved her passion and devotion to him. She would never let anything happen to him and she would always be there to hold his hand simply because she truly loved him with all of her soul.

Michelle and Marah immersed themselves in a plan to escape the preschool. They were exhausted and were finished with this project; every afternoon they kept making plans for a new business. They found a reliable competitor from their past communication equipment days and had a written agreement to distribute their products. They were so excited to open a new company, Tactical Mission Supply, and Michelle was anxious to present their business plan to Lasse.

# CHAPTER THIRTEEN

In March 2015 Michelle received an email from their family's favorite online Bible teacher. The email included a link to what he found to be a valuable documentary series, "The Truth About Cancer". Michelle watched the entire series and couldn't wait to share the information with Lasse, even though it had been eleven years since his prostate cancer treatment.

The first week of April Michelle landed in Charlotte, North Carolina on her way to visit Lasse in Jacksonville. They would have several days together and she couldn't wait to share the news about the business she and Marah had just opened. She was walking the terminals to kill the two hours she had to wait before boarding her flight to Jacksonville when she recognized her favorite Hebrew praise singer. He was at that time unknown, but his song, "Gadol Elohai" was the very one she and Marah sang every day in the preschool with the children. She dialed Marah on her cell phone.

"Marah! I think the singer of "Gadol Elohai" is sitting in one of those white rockers here in the Charlotte airport!"

"Get over there and say hello, Michelle!" Marah demanded excitedly.

"Oh, my word; I can't!"

"You get over there right now!"

Michelle walked over to the man with the guitar case and said, "Joshua?"

"Yes," he answered kindly with a huge smile.

"Oh my gosh!" she exclaimed. "I am so sorry to be a gushing granny but we sing "Gadol Elohai" every day in our preschool! We don't just sing it; it is the song we sing to God to praise Him every day!"

Joshua was absolutely endearing and even took a selfie with Michelle and posted it on his Facebook page. Then he took Michelle's phone and called Marah. They could not have been more blessed by that. Michelle would tell people how God had let her meet this man, who was virtually unknown at that time, but meant so much to her family; that it was a special blessing from the LORD to say she was doing okay.

When she landed in Jacksonville, Michelle flung herself into Lasse's arms and kissed him ravenously. She was so happy. But Lasse seemed moody and reserved. When they got to Green Cove Springs and had her suitcases and bags aboard Sixteen Tons, Lasse made some coffee. Michelle stowed her things and sat smiling at the flowers he had in his special "vase" on the table. He always had flowers for her but he put them in an empty plastic tub marked, "drill bits". Michelle cherished his quirky displays of love. She always left hidden but expected love notes on the boat when she headed home to Ohio. Only once she forgot and Lasse called her before she had left Jacksonville asking where she had hidden it. She loved that he looked for and kept all of her little love letters. She could never live without him.

Lasse turned from the galley and sat the mugs of French press coffee down on the table near the flowers. "I think I need to see the family doctor," he said matter-of-factly.

Michelle's brow wrinkled as she looked at him with immediate concern, "What's the matter?" she demanded.

"I have been having some bleeding in the toilet and things don't look as normal as they have for the last sixty eight years."

"Okay, I'll call Dr. Turner's office right now. Don't worry, Lover, it is probably just a hemorrhoid," Michelle said soothingly while calling their family doctor right then and getting an appointment for the end of the week. She hadn't realized that the cancer documentary series was going to be a sign of direction, a gift from Above, until a week later.

Lasse and Michelle rented a car in Green Cove Springs, Florida the next day and drove straight back to Ohio. Telling Lasse about the new company she had opened with Marah ended up being a rather deflated conversation than the hopeful news she had wanted it to be. She was sure he was overly worried and this was only a hemorrhoid problem. The man was in peak condition, ate homemade organic meals made with love along with fish and salad, he walked almost an hour daily; he was fine. He was strong and healthy, had plenty of fresh air and sunshine. He was fine, Michelle was sure of that.

Lasse had never had a colonoscopy and their family doctor said that would be the first step. Since they trusted the Cleveland hospital over any hospital in the Dayton area, Michelle once again relied on the help from Dr. John Smith. He gave them the name of the doctor he wanted Lasse to be seen by but the first available appointment wasn't for more two weeks.

"I want this looked at now!" Lasse roared. "I will not wait two more weeks! You get on that phone and find someone to see me as soon as possible." Fear had taken over Lasse. He never yelled.

"Okay, I will, but Lasse, I think we should see this doctor that Dr. Smith recommends. We may have to wait two weeks but if he is the best then that is who you have to see." Michelle tried to carefully get Lasse on track with seeing the best doctor but he wouldn't hear of it. He shouted more until she acquiesced and found Dr. Henry Miller who could see Lasse within the week. Michelle's heart sank. She felt they had been guided to the other doctor and fear was driving them instead of their faith. Michelle felt they were going in the wrong direction. She was right.

The next day they traded their older Toyota Avalon for a newer Volvo, a necessity for the many trips to Cleveland. They returned immediately to Green Cove Springs, had Sixteen Tons put on the hard (stored the boat in a cradle on the shore) in a tight lot in Tom Holland's shipyard, packed their bags, and headed to Cleveland.

They stayed in a hotel with the prescription bowel prep to be taken the night before the visit with Dr. Miller. In all their years together never had they mentioned any of the natural occurrences of the bowel. That may seem rather impossible but not for a noble lady nor for a former diplomat. No one in their family behaved like that except for their little grandson, Ivan, who was four years old and found himself quite entertaining. But the bowel prep in the small hotel room introduced them to an entirely different level of their relationship. They handled it beautifully, allowing for a few chuckles to ease their discomfort. This was the beginning of countless embarrassing moments for the both of them but their concern was for one another. Michelle would dash to protect Lasse's dignity and she would do whatever was needed to help him. This journey was not for the weak. Like Samwise Gamgee said about his best friend, Frodo, in "The Lord of the Rings", "I made a promise, Mr. Frodo, a promise. 'Don't you leave him, Samwise Gamgee.' And I don't mean to." Michelle never left Lasse's side. She held his hand through every hellish torture he was forced to endure. And it was hellish. They were going the wrong way.

The day they met Dr. Henry Miller he did a sigmoidoscopy while Michelle was in the room. He declared that Lasse definitely had colon cancer the very second he saw a small tumor and a couple of polyps. Michelle insisted on knowing how he had determined it was cancer and asked if there was any possibility that the tumor was benign. "Oh, no," Dr. Miller answered. "This is cancer. Mr. Paivola is the second man I have seen this morning who has a tumor very near of the spot where the radioactive seeds were placed in his prostate. It is most definitely malignant." Michelle wanted tests done before she would believe that but Lasse signed up for the protocol Dr. Miller prescribed. That happened within five minutes of putting his jeans back on. Dr. Miller's nurse, Susan, came into the room with two assistants. Lasse was to drive across town for the last MRI appointment of the day, then back to the hospital for bloodwork. He would see Dr. Johnson the next day, as well as Dr. Davis for radiation and Dr. Wilson for chemotherapy. Michelle begged Lasse to stop and reconsider, to get a second opinion. But he would not. He was going forward with this program and he was going to live through it. Michelle reminded Lasse of the statistics of mortality rate of people who took chemotherapy. He would not listen. She cried and begged him to at least think about it. He would not listen to her. Fear was driving him. Michelle was not convinced Lasse even had cancer but he sure was thrown into the three ring circus of surgery, chemotherapy, and radiation before they even had pathology on that small tumor.

In May all the preparations were made for the move to Hope Lodge, the Ronald McDonald House for adults in the Cleveland area. Michelle drove Lasse to Hope Lodge for an impromptu visit just to check it out. They saw a young man sitting in the foyer, weeping silently, bald and scabbed head bowed, while holding onto an IV pole. Oh Lord, this is not for us. Lasse declared, "I can't see someone suffering like that and have the faith to fight for myself. I don't want to live there."

Michelle sighed deeply and sadly, "Lasse, please, please reconsider this whole thing. Please get a second opinion." She begged him with all her heart and tears pooling in her desperate green eyes.

Lasse steeled his reserve, "No," he replied. "We will live at Hope Lodge and I will have chemo and radiation. Do not ask me again because this is the road I am taking."

And so, they moved to Cleveland. At Hope Lodge each patient must have a care giver; it is not a hospital or rehab, just a hotel-like group home. Each patient has a double queen suite with their own bathroom and a personal section of large case glass-doored refrigerators in the common area kitchen. There are also cupboards in the kitchen assigned to each patient. The care giver is expected to prepare all the meals for the patient and to clean up after using one of the three cooking areas. Michelle thought it was a lovely little concentration camp for those who had agreed to the tortures at the major hospitals in the area.

How Michelle hated Cleveland. She was born there and she was raised in the orphanage there. Cleveland was all bad memories for the little blonde haired girl with the sad green eyes. And now she was back. Nothing good had ever happened to her in Cleveland. Except for Dr. John Smith saving Lasse's life; so there was that one good thing. Cleveland made Michelle feel as if a dark cloak was pulled over her soul. She could hardly feel the warmth of the Light in that bleak place. How many tragedies had been forced upon that girl in Cleveland? The cruelty, the heartache, the abuse, the abandonment; dear God she hated that place. She had her Bible with her and she clung to God's promises of walking with them in the dark valley. And that is what Cleveland was to them.

They found helping others took their mind off their own problems and they befriended everyone. Lasse and Michelle were the most popular couple living at Hope Lodge during the six weeks of chemo and radiation that Lasse hoped would cure his cancer. Still beautiful and vibrant and devoted to one another, Lasse and Michelle attracted the saddest, sweetest people who found themselves listening intently to their love story. Michelle overheard one lady telling a couple of others, "And then he kissed her in the elevator!" Doctors and nurses also asked how the two had met and Lasse relished saying, "I thought she married me for love, but no, it was for revenge!" Michelle's devotion to Lasse dispelled any doubt of revenge and everyone could plainly see Lasse was the most beloved man.

They adjusted to life in the group home. They stocked their shelf in the refrigerator and their cupboard with items from the local Whole Foods grocery. Michelle prepared the healthiest meals from the only organic resource she could find. Lasse had purchased an expensive juicer and Michelle juiced organic fruits and vegetables for him. Lasse ate well, rested well, exercised well, and entertained everyone as people were just drawn to him. They involved themselves in the game nights and Lasse played Bingo for the first time. First time Bingo player, three time Bingo winner; of course! Twice a day Lasse and Michelle would walk at least three miles around the Little Italy neighborhood, faithfully avoiding the restaurants and bakeries. After the first month of this diligence they did cave to the bakeries and then nothing stopped them from trying every cannoli they found. It became a stress reliever to indulge in the sugary treats.

Their dearest friends were an Amish couple, Dave and Marie Yoder; and a mother and daughter from El Salvador, Carmen and Laura. The six of them were not that great at 1970's TV trivia but they were practically inseparable while living at Hope Lodge. Michelle took the ladies, Marie, who was a horse and buggy girl, Carmen, and Laura with only one leg, cruising in the Volvo to Whole Foods. The girls laughed their heads off and had a wonderful time. Michelle drove them out to Dave and Marie's farm and they were fascinated by the Amish lifestyle. They were precious friends that God had provided in the Valley of Weeping. They shared tears and laughter and knew the likelihood of all of them making it out of there alive was slim to none. Once when Michelle dissolved into hopeless tears, Carmen ordered, "You do not let the devil make you cry! Do not!" Michelle was so grateful for each of these women.

Lasse tolerated the chemo and radiation with only mild fatigue as a side effect. The doctors were well aware that he was working with Dr. Vanessa Adams, a naturopathic doctor in the Dayton area. The hospital doctors allowed certain supplements that she prescribed and they worked beautifully to protect his vitality.

Lasse only continued to be more attractive with age and there was one older nurse, nearing retirement, who did all she could to touch him. She was the chemotherapy nurse practitioner; Nurse Betty was her name. During one visit with Nurse Betty she insisted that Lasse could develop a rash and that she needed to check him all over to be sure his skin was intact.

Lasse said in his deep and charming accented voice, his blue eyes twinkling, "I don't have a rash, Ma'am."

Nurse Betty pressed further, "I will need to check to see if you have a diaper rash, Mr. Paivola."

"I assure you, I do not have a diaper or a diaper rash, Ma'am."

"Well, I am still required to check you, so Mrs. Paivola, please step out of the room and Mr. Paivola, please drop your pants."

Lasse was so pissed off at the violation and told the story many times of how that old lady gave his balls a good fondling. However, the next time she insisted that she needed to check his diaper rash, Lasse said, "No. No way." Michelle just grinned and offered to inspect his entire body any time he liked. Nurse Betty did not like being denied, nor did she appreciate their humor.

Even though mild fatigue was Lasse's main side effect of the chemo and radiation, sometimes he presented as if there was a bit more plaguing him. Once when he had his blood drawn, as he did weekly at the hospital, the male nurse returned with Lasse in a wheel-chair. Michelle was overwhelmed. "What's wrong?" she demanded desperately. He had walked back there fine just five minutes earlier.

"He felt a little dizzy after his blood was drawn; he is okay," the nurse assured her.

"I am fine. I don't need this wheelchair," Lasse said trying to get out of it.

"No, Sir, you will stay in this wheelchair. I am not going to get in trouble for allowing one of our patients to fall. Got that?" the nurse insisted.

"Lasse, are you okay?" Michelle fretted.

"I'm fine, Bambina, and I don't need this wheelchair. It is ridiculous."

Michelle adjusted Lasse's backpack, her purse, and his water bottle and tried to push the wheelchair. They managed a complete circle before the receptionist at the desk noted that the brake was still on. "Oh shoot," Michelle said.

Lasse did not find any of this amusing and Michelle was nervous about this first sign of Lasse's not being entirely well. Nothing could happen to her pirate husband. She was contemplating where to park as she wheeled him through scores of people all waiting to see their oncologists. She noticed a lonely wheelchair supporting a sleeping patient and headed in that direction. She tried to quietly parallel park next to the sleeping man but somehow got the large wheel on one side tangled with the sleeping man's wheel and no amount of back and forth maneuvers would free them. All of this was witnessed by the large crowd and Lasse was completely exasperated. He addressed the amused crowd with a shaking of his head and said, "Women drivers." He then ordered Michelle to just go ahead and push him down the nearby flight of stairs and get it over with. At least he didn't say, "In Finland you would get a ticket for that." When the nurse called Lasse's name there was nothing and no one who could stop him from rising out of that wheelchair and strutting confidently across the waiting room full of people.

Sometimes Hope Lodge was visited by orchestras and the patients were treated to the most amazing music. Dear Lord,

Michelle thought, could that really be the Leonore Overture from Beethoven's Fidelio they were playing? How appropriate, she concluded as she once again compared this entire episode in their lives as a trip through a concentration camp, a very comfortable and pretty concentration camp. How much she hated Dr. Henry Miller's voice. The hard German accent prodded her imaginings of Lasse behind the enemy lines while she tried desperately to find a way of escape for him. She knew with all her being this was not the right path to save Lasse's life. Dear God, they were going the wrong direction; this was all wrong.

Lasse and Michelle returned home in mid-June 2015 and Lasse seemed very well. Dr. Miller had scheduled the "big" surgery for September. This meant that he would use the Da Vinci robot to remove the shrinking tumor and part of Lasse's large intestine, and then he would create a temporary ileostomy while the resection of colon and intestine healed. "I can say that Mr. Paivola will most likely have five more years if he completes our protocol with the surgery," Dr. Miller said. Michelle heard something along the lines of, "Arbeit macht frei." She began to loathe this man and everything about him. Who did he think he was giving a five year limit on Lasse's life? How dare he? He did not have the authority to put a time stamp on Lasse. Every time Lasse and Michelle met with Dr. Miller she felt that he was pushing them hard, shoving them in the wrong direction. She feared that Dr. Miller's plan was going to do more harm than good. She was right.

Lasse intuitively knew that things may not go as he had hoped. He insisted they sell their dream home because if he should die or be incapacitated with health issues, Michelle wouldn't be able to even change the lightbulbs in the eighteen foot ceilings in the living room. She would never be able to take care of that big house and without life insurance she would never be able to afford it. For her good, he needed to get her to a more manageable home. They spent the summer packing, having a garage sale and giving away most everything, putting their things into storage units, and preparing the house for sale.

Jere, Lasse's oldest son, came from Finland for a week's visit and on the way to pick him up from the airport they received a call that a buyer had made an offer on their home. This home where their lives had been joyous and full of love and adventure and parties and laughter and family visits and a prosperous business was now offered to another family. Michelle wanted to let the pent up tears flow but not yet. Jere was here. He would help her save Lasse and that was all that was important at the moment. They would make happy memories in another house, right?

Their realtor found half a dozen homes for them to look at, all of them a quarter of the size of their huge, family home. Jere gave constructive advice and they all agreed upon a small brick ranch on the south end of town. It was sixty years old, built to last, and full of the 1950's charm. It was solid and had a wood burning fireplace with an updated kitchen and bathroom. Lasse determined that Michelle could manage this house. Before their purchase was complete, though, it was time for surgery.

# CHAPTER FOURTEEN

Michelle hosted a huge birthday party for Lasse the weekend before they left for the surgery in Cleveland. They gathered together on their large deck that was filled with colorful, hardy fall mums, bales of straw, and pumpkins. She had prepared a long dinner table, brought out the dining room chairs, and put Lasse's favorite antique amber glass lanterns on the table draped in linen. There was music and homemade food and pies and hugs and laughter and singing. This gathering of family and friends helped to bolster Lasse's spirit, because although he stated vehemently that he was not afraid, he was. He didn't want to die or to have an ileostomy but he wanted this cancer gone. He loved his life and he was grateful for it. He loved this lady who gave him a hand to hold through it all and found ways to honor him and show him how much she cherished him. But he was afraid. He prayed repeatedly that God would forgive him in all the ways he had erred against Him.

Dr. Miller had assured Lasse and Michelle that everything would go well. But it didn't. Michelle had to have Lasse at the hospital's surgery center by 5am for the surgery prep and the surgery itself was to last about seven hours. During the prep Michelle helped Lasse to get his clothes into the hospital bags and to get his gown on as instructed. She gave his buttocks a squeeze and tied up the gown. Lasse turned and hugged her briefly then hopped onto the hospital bed. The nurses came and administered part of the pre-surgery drugs and the IV. Michelle kissed Lasse repeatedly and whispered little prayers over him, encouraging him that the Lord had always taken care of him. She kissed him sweetly and smiled into his eyes one last time, willing him with all her being to come back to her, and then they wheeled his bed down the hall.

Michelle was directed to the surgery waiting room where she pulled her Bible out of her tote and began to read and pray for Lasse. "Heavenly Father, do You take care of my Lasse? Please, God, don't let anything happen to him. I need him, Father."

Thirteen hours later Dr. Miller came to speak with Michelle. She tried not to hate him. There had been an issue with a loose brachytherapy seed which prevented them being able to insert a catheter until an ultrasound had been done. Once that was taken care of, the surgery did take longer than expected. Yes, he was under anesthesia for much longer than was wanted but he should be okay. Forty centimeters of colon was removed. "Wait, what? Forty centimeters? Why forty? The tumor was three centimeters, why did you take forty centimeters of his large colon?" Michelle demanded.

"We take forty centimeters from everyone because that is our standard procedure, Mrs. Paivola," Dr. Miller answered patiently with a deep tiredness he was unable to hide.

"But that is where most nutrition is absorbed. Lasse is not standard. Okay, go on, what else?" Michelle was angry, frustrated, and fearful.

Dr. Miller continued to give a brief explanation of the ileostomy and said that he would see Lasse tomorrow during his hospital rounds. He expected Lasse to do very well.

As soon as Lasse was stable Michelle was allowed back in the recovery room. He lifted his gown and looked down at the clear bag attached to a small loop of gut that was now exposed through a hole in his skin. He examined all the hoses and tubes and drains, then looked at Michelle for her reaction. She steadied herself and looked into Lasse's eyes, love and concern transmitted without a word. Lasse gave her a thumbs up and demanded she take a picture with her phone.

"It's going to be okay, Lover," she told him. "You're alive and we will figure this stoma thing out. We'll be okay. Thank God you're alive – oh my gosh, it took so long." Then Michelle proceeded to tell Lasse all that Dr. Miller had explained to her. The man had just come out of a thirteen hour surgery and was demanding to know everything that had happened to him. Yeah, that pirate husband was going to be just fine.

As Lasse was wheeled through the halls of the hospital and taken up to the gut ward, as Michelle called it, he became more alert. He insisted he was ready to walk before they even had his monitors hooked up. He tried charming the nurses but they told him he could wait until morning to walk even though they could tell he was ready. When they were alone again Lasse opened his gown and they both took a closer look at that stoma. Michelle's brow furrowed with concern. Lord God, there is a gut hanging out, she thought. It made her a bit woozy to look at it but Lasse was alive and she could only thank God for that. She would deal with whatever hell was dished out as long as Lasse was alive.

The next morning Lasse was allowed to walk and he made several rounds on the unit. He was attached to an IV pole that included a pain pump, a pain pump that he was not using. Lasse had a very high tolerance for pain and the less pain medicine he used the better for his clarity to fight it mentally. This was going to be the catalyst of a major problem within the week. There was a young man walking with his girlfriend who had his entire guts removed and Lasse outrageously challenged the boy to a race. He won of course by three laps; of course he did, forty-five years the boy's senior meant nothing to Lasse. He would win or he would cry and win, and he won. Michelle chuckled at Lasse and apologized to the young couple. Lasse and Michelle wondered out loud together if the two would marry and could that boy ever have children and a normal life after what had been done to him.

Dr. Miller stopped in Lasse's room for all of thirty-seven seconds and declared Lasse's surgery a success and said things were proceeding so well that he expected Lasse to go home on the fifth day after surgery. This was the plan but they were still there after three weeks and a near death experience.

Lasse had started to eat and things had begun to pass through the ileostomy. That was as planned. Lasse continued to walk and increased his rounds of the unit all throughout the day. But he wasn't using the pain pump. The stoma nurse had come by and said it was time for Michelle to learn to change the stoma bag. When the bag was removed and the intestinal loop was exposed without its plastic covering, Michelle stared at it, focusing in on the real life fact that

Lasse's guts which were supposed to be inside were now hanging on the outside. The room began to blur and all sounds were very far away for Michelle and the nurse quickly put her in a chair. "Listen, you are going to be the one handling the stoma bags and changing this for your husband. You will have to get used to this. I'll change it this time but the next time I come, you'll be the one changing it." Michelle took slow, deep breaths and the reoccurring thought was, there's a gut hanging out of Lasse. She needed some fortitude to be able to help him. She would do it or she would cry and do it but she would do this for him. Michelle had taken to measuring the output of every drain as well as his urine output through the catheter. She squeezed the drain that would fill with blood from his abdomen and then she would measure and empty it. She dumped his urine and blood and kept track of every ounce of output. She could learn the stoma as well. She would do anything for Lasse, anything.

The next time the stoma nurse came, Michelle swallowed hard and kept her eyes on the nurse and the cleaning gauze and the new stoma bag. She kept her eyes averted from the actual stoma and no, neither of them wanted to name it as some patients do. This was a temporary thing and not a cute new life partner or pet. The nurse swabbed the stoma and it became active. She said that happens and you just have to deal with it and that some people will just get in the shower until the episode passes. This meant that bile and liquid feces was coming out through the stoma. Both Lasse and Michelle felt mortified but this was their new, although temporary, normal and they would get through it together. It was just a chapter in their lives, not the whole story. The stoma was working and for that they had to be grateful.

After the fifth day Dr. Miller came by to say that it was now time to remove Lasse's pain pump and that he could go home the next day since he was eating and the stoma was working well. A nurse came in shortly afterwards, removed the pain pump, and handed Lasse two Dilaudid. This was to replace the pain pump medication; the pain pump that Lasse had not been using. This narcotic caused Lasse's stoma to become inactive, it in fact, paralyzed his gut and the nightmare began. It did not take but the next twenty-four hours before Lasse's gut began to swell and he started to feel really badly. This brought in nurses with more Dilaudid and more swelling of his gut which no longer functioned at all. He could not go home.

Dr. Miller came by two days later and said he did not understand why Lasse had begun to swell when things had been functioning perfectly. No one suspected the Dilauded. Lasse's discomfort increased and Michelle paced the room. There were no answers to help him. Dear Lord, she prayed over and over.

Day then night, then day Lasse just became sicker and sicker. He closed his eyes and breathed slowly and said, "Bambina, I am sorry."

"You have nothing to be sorry about, Lover. Just please, please get better. Please." Michelle begged.

"That is what I try to do." In the next instant Lasse muttered, "I am going to throw up."

Michelle grabbed the trash can and the liquid shit that should have traveled out through his stoma was now being projectile vomited into the large trash can she was holding. She grabbed paper towels and wiped Lasse's face and beard. "Oh, my darling, I am so sorry this is happening to you," she cried.

Michelle pushed the nurse call button and eventually someone showed up. A resident ordered an NG tube to pump the contents of Lasse's stomach so he would not vomit and possibly damage his stoma or tear his resected colon. The kind, young Russian nurse assigned to them that evening said to Lasse with serious intent, "Sir, if you want this NG tube, you need to let me be the one to put it in." It was actually a protective warning that both of them missed.

"I don't want it." Lasse was not willing to have the NG tube inserted into his nostril, down the back of his throat, and into his stomach.

The nurse looked at him, her big blue eyes tender with concern and said, "Okay."

But the puking came back and Michelle was catching it with the trash can and wiping the fecaloid vomit from his beard and helping him to rinse his mouth.

The resident who ordered the NG tube stopped in Lasse's room on her way out of the hospital for the evening to see how the placement had gone. She was furious when she saw that her orders had not been followed. She threw her winter coat off, grabbed the NG tubing and began shoving it into Lasse's nostril. Michelle pushed the nurse call button and the young Russian girl came running in and shouted, "No, wait, stop, you can't do it like that!" The resident was ramming the tube and Lasse began gagging and vomiting everywhere.

Michelle sobbed out loud to watch her husband being tortured and injured by people they had blindly trusted to help him. "God! Help him please!" she prayed out loud while bawling. She heaved great sobs as the Russian nurse assisted the resident and got the NG tube placed in the other nostril, the one that wasn't blocked.

The resident came over to Michelle, put her hand on her shoulder, and said sweetly, "He is going to be okay, Mrs. Paivola." Michelle was seething and could not reply. I will kill you, she thought viciously. I will fucking kill you. The Russian nurse tended to Lasse gently and Michelle cried while helping to get his bedding and gown changed. Lasse began to calm down and the pumping began, the first of six, one and a half liter canisters quickly filled. Lasse drifted off into a very deep sleep. Michelle held his hand, tucked him in, made sure he was as comfortable as possible, and laid her head on his bed and prayed. In her heart she heard the words of Betsy ten Boom to her sister, Corrie. After Betsy had been assaulted and badly beaten by a Nazi guard in Ravensbruck concentration camp for being too slow to carry boulders when she was very ill, Corrie went mad and was ready to avenge her sister. Betsy reached her badly bruised hand towards her protective sister and said, "Don't hate, Corrie, don't hate." God, how will I not hate these people for what they have done to Lasse? "Don't hate, Corrie, don't hate." How? How will I do that? she prayed.

Lasse did not move for two days and two nights. Michelle had not left for Hope Lodge to shower in days. They were in Cleveland and their family was so far away from them. They offered to drive there and help but Michelle always said, "Not yet, maybe tomorrow." They were all deeply concerned and willing to come there. Michael and Christopher were ready to burn that hospital to the ground for how badly Lasse was being treated. Marah continually prayed and sent words of encouragement and love. Marianne, Lasse's daughter, offered to fly from Finland.

On the first day of the NG tube nightmare Lasse hadn't moved and Michelle asked the nurse, "Is he going to be okay? Why isn't he waking up? Is he going to live?" She was demanding answers now.

"Oh, he is okay; he is just sleeping."

"Sleeping?" she asked incredulously. "He can't even hear me when I speak to him and he doesn't even notice when his blood is drawn. Why isn't he waking up?"

"His body is very tired from all it has been through. He will be okay. He is just sleeping."

Michelle did not trust anyone at this point. She told one nurse, "We are not the family that believes in lawsuits. We will just get your address." She told every doctor to take the best care of Lasse because, "After God, he is most important to me." This was the truth. Her soul was seared into his and she could not live without him. She was bound to him; he was her life.

When Dr. Miller stood at the doorway and wouldn't come to Lasse's bed during his "just sleeping" days, Michelle demanded, "Would you please come in and look at him? What is wrong with him?"

Dr. Miller chuckled nervously and entered the room but not too close to Lasse. "He is just resting, Mrs. Paivola. I will be back tomorrow and we will see how he is then."

A storm of curse words and vicious thoughts filled Michelle's mind. On the inside she was screaming every word and threat but outwardly she was bristling silently; there was no doubt Dr. Miller understood her thoughts.

During the last night of Lasse's deep sleep he began to pull the covers with his left hand and then his right hand was moving as if he was writing. He did this over and over and Michelle decided to record a video on her phone so she could ask him later.

The next day Lasse slowly came awake and Michelle brushed his hair with her hands and kissed his face and whispered to him that she was so grateful he was alive. The NG tube was still pumping and it was extremely uncomfortable for Lasse. His body did not accept this foreign object and began to create mucous that he coughed and choked on. Michelle helped him to cough and spit the mucous out and then she wiped that from his beard with a warm wash cloth. She was tender in all her efforts to help him.

Lasse took tiny sips of water, since the NG tube was just going to pump it out anyway, but it helped to soothe his throat some. He told her, "Bambina, I saw something."

"What, Lover? What did you see?"

"I am not saying I 'went toward the light' but everything around me was bright white. I got a better understanding of God and the Bible. I started to laugh while I was in this bright white because it was so simple. I laughed and was happy and I thought I had better write this down or I am going to forget it. Listen, it is so simple to follow God."

"Oh, my Love, that is beautiful. And Lasse! You were writing! You were writing while you were sleeping the last two days! How beautiful!"

They held hands and Michelle kissed Lasse tenderly on the cheek being very careful not to bump his nose where the NG tube was taped and hurting.

"Oh dear God, You are so good to us. Thank You for this message to Lasse, that You accept him, that he is Your child, and that it truly is so simple to follow You. Thank You, thank You that he woke up, oh, thank You, Father!" Michelle could not have been more grateful. She was so grateful.

Another day passed with the NG tube and Lasse was completely alert. He insisted, "Michelle, go to Hope Lodge and take a shower, you must." She did not want to leave him but it had been several days already so she quickly left and returned as soon as possible. The trip to Hope Lodge had brought love and concern from their friends and many inquiries, "How is Lasse?" they all wanted to know.

"Not very well," was Michelle's grave answer. They promised to keep praying for him and Michelle was so grateful that they had been blessed with these precious friends.

More mucous formed until Lasse spent a good deal of the day and night choking on it. There was concern for pneumonia and he was taken for an x-ray but that showed his lungs were clear. Michelle pulled the thick mess Lasse was choking on from out of his throat and mouth; she cleaned his beard, kissed his cheek, and prayed fervently for him.

Once the NG tube was removed the mucous began to clear and it was time to see if eating and stoma output would resume. None of this was an easy process and Michelle watched every hand that touched Lasse, guarding him from any harm. In a few days things began to slowly improve and a little output was coming through the stoma.

It seemed that just when things looked better they would get really bad really fast. One night a nurse named, Cindy, was on duty. She was about Michelle's age and had short, spikey, purplish-red hair. She introduced herself politely enough but it soon became clear that she was not concerned about helping Lasse. Lasse refused any more narcotics for pain and so when he told her he was feeling some pain and pressure in his lower abdomen she told him it was normal with the surgery.

"Bambina, I can't take this pain," Lasse told Michelle, his agony clearly being translated through his strained voice. "It feels like something is tearing apart inside me."

Michelle pushed the nurse call button, which she only did if Lasse had a problem she could not take care of herself. They both knew that you had better not annoy those who held your life in their hands. But Cindy appeared and she was annoyed. It seemed that she felt that if Lasse was going to refuse narcotics then pain was a consequence of what she thought was a poor decision.

"Mr. Paivola, you are fine. It is just some pressure you are feeling. I have run the bladder scanner over you and you only have 5ml of urine in your bladder. You are going to be fine. Just try to go to sleep." She dismissed herself without an ounce of empathy.

For the next couple of hours Lasse writhed in pain and Michelle worried immensely without a hope of help. She prayed over him and held his hand and worried but did not know what else to do. She pushed the nurse call button and a very young nurse aide came into their room. Michelle explained that Lasse was tough, he knew pain, he had been shot twice, stabbed multiple times, and beaten with a baseball bat; he understood how to deal with pain. The nurse aide said, "I will run this bladder scanner over him again," then she paused. "Oh my gosh. This has been on the child setting. You have 700ml of urine in your bladder. Mr. Paivola, try to stand to pee and maybe the gravity will help force it out."

Michelle helped Lasse into the bathroom and he did pee, only he was near collapsing and so Michelle sat him on the toilet. His pain was excruciating as one of the metal pins that had been used to hold his resected colon to his rectum passed through him and out into the toilet. Michelle's heart broke as she held Lasse upright in her arms and he trembled with pain that was out of control. He leaned against her body and clung to her, his breathing labored with all the waves of torment that passed over and through him.

"Oh, God, please help us," Michelle prayed as she cried.

The nurse aide called for the nurse as Michelle was putting Lasse back into bed. Michelle took a picture of the pin at the bottom of the toilet bowl that was tinged with Lasse's blood.

"Oh, Mr. Paivola, you did have to pee!" Cindy exclaimed but no apologies came with the mistake that had cost Lasse more than one night of pain. This night of pain from that one mistake would continue to the end of Lasse's life.

"Oh, Lasse, we have to get out of here," Michelle whispered as she kissed his cheek and prayed over him.

A couple of hours later, it was nearing dawn and Lasse suffered continuously, he breathed, "Bambina, something is happening with my rectum. Will you please check?"

"Oh, dear God...," Michelle gasped. There was enough blood filling the bed from his rectum to have been from a birth. She opened their door which was front and center of the nurses' station and called for Cindy to come immediately.

Cindy was shocked and instantly her demeanor was for helping Lasse. "No, this isn't normal, Mr. Paivola." Michelle helped to change the bedding but kept the sheet protector full of blood to show Dr. Miller later that morning.

When Dr. Miller arrived that morning and read the report, he said, "Sometimes this happens; don't worry about it, Mr. Paivola." Michelle was so pissed off with Dr. Miller's cavalier attitude towards something that even Nurse Cindy had said was not normal. Someone was wrong, dead wrong.

"So," Michelle said glaringly at Dr. Miller, "we are not supposed to worry about this amount of blood?" She opened the sheet protector to show just how much blood Lasse had lost. "This is normal, huh?"

"I know, it looks like a lot of blood but he is going to be okay, Mrs. Paivola."

"He better be." Michelle threatened. Inside she heard Betsy ten Boom, "Don't hate, Corrie, don't hate." But she did hate. She hated Dr. Miller and Cindy and the resident who harmed Lasse with the NG tube. She hated this hospital and Cleveland and cancer and stupid mistakes. She hated the fear that had driven them to think this path would be their salvation and it was all a big mistake.

"I am prescribing Flowmax to help Mr. Paivola's urinary output. That will help solve any issues and the bleeding will stop. No worries, Mrs. Paivola, he is going to be okay."

Well, that was something too good to hope for as Lasse's equilibrium became unbalanced. After two and a half weeks of being hospitalized Lasse could no longer stand without passing out. Dr. Miller ordered physical therapy nurses to bring a walker for him. Michelle was outraged.

"This man is a 15,000 FitBit steps a day guy. He doesn't need a damn walker! He needs someone to figure out why he is passing out!"

It was the Flowmax. Dr. Miller decided it would be better for Lasse to heal at home. Michelle was able to change the stoma dressings and bag so they decided to bolt for the door now that Dr. Miller had given them permission. Michelle held Lasse, her arms wrapped tightly around his waist, as he hardly walked to their room at Hope

Lodge. They would stop every few steps and he would breathe and try to remain conscious.

After resting a few hours on the bed in their room at Hope Lodge Lasse said he felt somewhat steadier and insisted Michelle get him into the shower. He had lost thirty pounds over the last month and he looked like a scarecrow.

"Lover, why don't you just let me give you another sponge bath? You don't need to get into the shower. It is dangerous."

"No. I want to shower. I want to feel clean. Help me get these clothes off."

She sighed and, as always, Michelle did as she was ordered by Lasse. He groaned with joy as she washed his hair with baby shampoo, then scrubbed his back and arms and legs. She turned the water off, patted his skin dry with a large, white towel, then she wrapped it around his body. Lasse placed his right arm around Michelle's neck as he lifted a leg out of the tub and then everything went spotty and black for him. He passed out in her arms.

"Lasse!" Michelle shouted. "You will not do this! Wake up! You cannot fall!" All of Lasse's weight was on her and it was a good thing he had wrapped an arm around her. She was strong. She held him. She would not let him fall. She stretched as far as she could and reached the sink counter with her free arm and put some of her homemade peppermint baking soda toothpaste on her finger. She ran it over Lasse's gums, hoping to revive him with the peppermint. "Thank You, God," she breathed as Lasse began to regain consciousness. She mostly carried him back to the bed and gently laid him down.

"Oh, darling Lasse!" she exclaimed. "We have to get you better!" Michelle began to cry with relief that she had not dropped

Lasse and that he had not been injured. "Oh, thank You, thank You, God," she prayed repeatedly.

"Bambina," he breathed. "Thank you." Michelle laid down beside Lasse and cried with helplessness. She could carry Lasse but she didn't know how to fix him. She couldn't fix him and dread filled her soul. Lasse was weak, he continued to have a birth-like bleeding episode every single morning for the next seven weeks. She did not know what to do.

Lasse could have some semi-solid foods, he practiced walking in the room, and regained a little strength. Michelle had to measure all the output of the stoma and record it for Dr. Miller; this happened several times a day and she became regimented in her duties to serve and protect Lasse.

Seated on the closed lid of the toilet after having eaten some Mexican dinner that had been served to all at Hope Lodge, Lasse steadied himself as Michelle knelt on the floor to open the stoma bag.

"Holy shit that stinks!" Lasse proclaimed in disgust. Michelle cracked up at his words but kept working quickly to empty, measure, and flush away the contents of the bag.

"Open the window, Bambina!" Lasse ordered.

"Lover, you know that is against the rules at Hope Lodge. We are not allowed to open the windows because the pollen may harm someone whose immune system is compromised."

"Open it right now or I am going to die of this smell!"

And, of course, Michelle did exactly as Lasse ordered. She had often said, "You know, it is a good thing you're not a drug addict because I end up doing everything you order me to do!"

During this stay Michael, Christopher, and Marah had emptied the family home of all its contents and prepared everything for Lasse and Michelle in the house they had found just before the surgery. The kids did everything for them. Christopher had been in a meeting at the local community college where he worked and his boss noticed the worry on his face. "Chris, what's wrong?" Evan asked right in the middle of the meeting.

"My step-dad's not doing too well," he said in a strained but steeled voice.

"What can we do to help?" Evan asked. Christopher's coworkers headed over to Lasse and Michelle's new home, ready to work. They removed all the old carpeting and put it out for the trash.

Marah's entire family showed up to help with sanding the wood floors, cleaning the walls, ceilings, windows, and closets. Michael came with Audrey, his step-daughter, to help move them in. Marah's mom helped to move all the dishes and place them in the freshly cleaned kitchen cabinets, and then she stocked the refrigerator. Marah arranged a moving party with family, friends, and neighbors. Little Ivan oversaw all the work and placed his stuffed Snoopy on the bed for Poppi to come home to. They lit the fire in the fireplace and waited for their homecoming. All that Lasse and Michelle had to do was come in and survive. Has anyone ever been so blessed? So well taken care of? It was almost heaven to settle by the fire with their family. They had survived and escaped Cleveland.

The birth-like rectal bleeding continued every day for a full seven weeks before Dr. Miller decided, that, "No, it has not healed. Come in and I will surgically insert a mushroom drain that will help it." And so, another trip to Cleveland was made, another promise that this would be a simple procedure, another promise broken, and more suffering for Lasse. This particular surgery was called a hemorrhoid removal but it was really all about covering up mistakes that were made. The doctor had inserted the drain into Lasse's rectum but had sewn the thing to Lasse's buttock. The man could not move without pulling stitches. Both Lasse and Michelle were angry, however, Lasse kept his cool whereas Michelle fumed with a rage that was always at a low boil.

Regardless of how bad he felt, Lasse trained and strengthened himself. His first walk was to the end of the driveway and back. That was all the further he could make. But by the end of the week he was walking to the stop sign, then to the end of the block. He continued to push himself and soon he was walking around the block.

While he pushed himself daily, Michelle created soups and homemade bread for him. She busied herself in the kitchen chopping carrots, onions, and celery to add to butternut squash or sweet potatoes or pumpkin for soups. Lasse devoured the food and although it took a couple of months, he was strong and back to his normal weight. She made his favorite dish of boiled cod and a white cream sauce as often as he wished. He told her it was as good as his mother's, and whether it was or not, Michelle was pleased that he loved it.

Michelle was in charge of keeping all stoma supplies stocked, as well as changing out the sealant ring and bag every two days. It was always a big production that required a step by step process with all supplies at hand. Lasse would wait impatiently on the bed for her to use the special ointment that removed the sealed ring, she would dispose of the ring and bag while he quickly showered, hoping that the stoma would not become active while open to the air. Michelle would then use the hair dryer to make sure his skin was dry so that the glue would completely seal the new ring and bag. It was a process but she was careful so that his skin would never break out with a rash or get infected.

Lasse dreamed of heading to Florida to visit his beloved boat, Sixteen Tons, but had to accept that he could not travel that far by car yet. He was receiving updates from his boating friends in Green Cove Springs but he missed his girl. He was grumpy and impatient to get back to living.

The plan had been to have the ileostomy reversal three months post-surgery and then begin a new round of heavy duty chemotherapy. Because of the episode with his bladder and the tearing of the resected colon, leading to the seven weeks of heavy bleeding and the mushroom drain, now they had to wait for the reversal. Lasse was being instructed to begin the chemotherapy without the reversal. This just tore at Michelle's soul.

"Why? Why do you need that kind of heavy duty chemo when you do not have any cancer in your body? I think it is wrong and you need another opinion."

"In case they missed something with the surgery, microscopic cancer cells – that is why."

"All of your bloodwork shows that you are cancer free, Lasse. That shit causes cancer! Please."

Lasse became sullen and was determined to see the next phase through. He was disgusted with the ileostomy and he wanted to get the four months of intravenous chemotherapy behind him so he could get the reversal surgery. He just wanted to feel like himself again and not have this shit bag hanging on him all the time. All the fucking struggles could pile up on him at once if he knew he would live. He had only the advice of Dr. Miller, Dr. Wilson, and Dr. Davis from Cleveland. Dr. Wilson told him since the chemotherapy would be delivered to his system over a period of forty-eight hours for many months that he may as well have the treatment close to home. He recommended Dr. John Brown in Dayton.

Michelle did as Lasse ordered and set up the appointment with Dr. Brown, who turned out to be a very compassionate man. It was hard not to like or trust him, but Michelle didn't trust the entire American cancer treatment industry. She believed completely that they were still on the wrong path and that although Dr. Brown was nice, he was still selling his own program of chemotherapy poisons. Lasse liked Dr. Brown immediately. He agreed to start the treatment at the beginning of January. Michelle still implored Dr. Brown to explain why Lasse needed chemotherapy when there was no evidence of cancer in his body.

"Seriously, Dr. Brown, why are we going to take chemotherapy when all of his bloodwork is normal? He had one small tumor and I have never even heard that there was proof that it was malignant. Why does he need this treatment right now?"

"It is standard procedure to finish this part of the protocol for fighting cancer. He has to have the chemotherapy to be certain that all the cancer is out of his body."

All Michelle heard was bull shit; she didn't believe Dr. Brown for a moment. "Dear God, please protect Lasse from these poisons." She was absolutely certain only harm could come from this standard protocol. Pouring toxins into his perfectly healthy body was ludicrous. She believed they should walk away, no, that they should run away. She was right.

But Lasse moved forward with the chemotherapy, Michelle fretted and made all the appointments for him. She prayed over him when the chemotherapy port was surgically placed on the right side of his chest. She sat with him while the poisons were pumped through that port. She helped him into the bathroom at home with the chemo pump that coursed poison through his system for forty-eight hours every two weeks for months. Lasse was hopeful but worried and Michelle was disgusted and worried. The chemotherapy was finished by mid-May 2016 and the ileostomy reversal surgery was scheduled for July.

During the chemotherapy treatments Lasse began to worry about everything; he was feeling out of control of his life. His frustrations and worry boiled over onto Michelle. These roller coaster emotions were not like him but still Michelle was wounded by his words and actions. Her sister, Heather, had suggested she write out a prayer to keep in her pocket.

She wrote on a photo of Lasse, "This is your husband – he is calm, cool, and collected. Be patient while his storms are raging. He promised he will always come back. Love is patient. Love is kind. Love does not hold a grudge. Love covers a multitude of raging storms. Stop reacting and respond with calm assurance. I have found the one whom my soul loves. Look at those lips! Oh my gosh – remember him as he truly is and not as this broken man trying to regain his life. Love is patient. Love is kind. Love remembers no wrongs. Look at that beautiful nose! Oh my word – it is perfect. Be patient. Be kind. Forget these storms and look forward to a better day."

A friend of Michelle's had opened a small tax office and hired her as his secretary for the afternoons and evenings. This allowed her to take Lasse to chemo in the mornings, get him back home, and then still have a part time job. She was babysitting a little girl before and after school and she also took a part time job as a tour guide at the local career tech school, as well as taught preschool on Fridays at Dayton Christian. She kept buying organic food and making the homemade soups and bread because it was best for Lasse. Could her circus have more rings? She jumped through all the hoops with a smile for everyone but her heart was crushed by Lasse's constantly fluctuating emotions. Prayer always calmed her and her specific prayer for Lasse held her together.

The chemotherapy treatments ended that May. Lasse had to wait a few weeks to clear his system of chemo and then he and Michelle traveled again to Cleveland for the reversal. Dr. Miller performed the surgery. In the hospital, Lasse did all he could to get back to eating and making sure his gut was working properly. He avoided all the pain medication offered to him except for Tylenol. All seemed in functioning order and they were released from the hospital.

For whatever reasons, reversals can affect people differently. For Lasse the nightmarish eliminations began right away. Immediately when they got home Lasse began his thirty trips a day to the toilet. It was all painful and exhausting. Worse yet, there was no information on how to slow down the number of bowel movements and the only advice from the Cleveland hospital was, "Your body will figure it out." Lasse found a British protocol that suggested a shot of prune juice, a large meal, followed with a big mug of hot coffee and lots of Imodium that could help him control his system and get the trips to the toilet down to about six per day. So, even though Lasse was free from the ileostomy bag, he was not free to even leave the house.

Within days of returning from Cleveland a raging infection began at the surgical site and inside his body. Michelle sent pictures to Dr. Miller's nurse but was assured that the hot pink lumpiness was all a normal part of healing. It wasn't. Michelle took Lasse to the emergency room of the best Dayton area hospital where he was admitted until the puss-leaking infection was cleared up. Lasse suffered continually with the thirty trips to the toilet even at the hospital and Michelle did whatever she had to, making sure her pirate husband could retain all the dignity possible in this horrific situation. Lasse thanked Michelle profusely and apologized; she told him to shut up because he would do the same for her. But she cried, knowing none of this was right.

# CHAPTER FIFTEEN

---◦◦◦---

It took nearly three months for healing but as soon as Lasse was strong enough, he armed himself with lots of Imodium, loaded up the car, and headed for Florida to work on Sixteen Tons. Michelle felt lost in life without him; he was her reason for everything and she lived to serve him. It was back to preparing freezer meals for his life on the boat but now she didn't know what to do with her own life. She was exhausted and recovering from the trauma of the last year.

That fall while Lasse was gone to the boat, Michelle continued babysitting before and after school, and her job as a tour guide at the local career tech school, as well as teaching at Dayton Christian on Fridays. These jobs weren't meant as a career but served their purpose so at the least notice she could take care of Lasse if needed. There would be plenty of time to plan her next career when Lasse was fully well.

Once a month Michelle would pack up Daisy, their old lady miniature tea-cup Chihuahua, and head to Florida for long week-ends with Lasse. Sitting together on the bow deck of Sixteen Tons one evening before a storm, Lasse and Michelle discussed and carved out Lasse's plans for the next decade. Sixteen Tons was still on the hard, upheld from the ground by iron rods, in Tom Holland's shipyard but she was still a livable residence.

"So, you're telling me you want to sell this boat and buy a sailboat to make a trip across the Atlantic?"

"Yes! First I will sail from the East Coast to the Azores Islands, you can fly there and we will have a mini vacation – although they say it is very windy there," Lasse continued. His eyes lit up with excitement and his passion for living and adventure was evident in the richness of his voice.

Michelle shook her head. When was this pirate ever going to settle down at home? He said they would buy a mini farm and she could have her mini sheep and a vineyard and he would have seven dogs, as well as raise her hobby chickens. She had plans for Lasse to build her a fancy-schmancy hen house. He had promised her he would do it. When was that going to happen? Not for a while it seemed.

The wind was blowing hard and whipped Michelle's blonde hair into her eyes and mouth, across her face. She repeatedly pushed it back uselessly and took a sip of the cabernet sauvignon Lasse had carried out to her. It was only recently that they had even begun to drink wine. All of Lasse's doctors had said it would be good for him and so they would share a glass each evening.

Michelle observed the riggings beating against the masts on the nearby boats. The wind carried tiny bits of dirt and sand that sometimes stung her face. A storm was blowing into northeast Florida from the west across the Gulf but the rain hadn't arrived yet. Terns were taking advantage of the increasingly fierce winds, coasting for enjoyment while offering their harsh, shrill calls so that all would notice their dare-devil escapades on the gusts that carried them higher. Michelle smiled at them, thinking, her pirate husband was like those birds, thrilling at the hope of adventure.

"Fine. I will meet you there, Lasse Paivola, but I want to see the whole place – every island, flower, path, and shop. I am not going to live without you for months at a time without some kind of reward. You are always leaving me without a hand to hold. You and your adventures cost me years of my life, you know?"

"Yes, Bambina! You will see it all and we will continue on together from Azores to the fishing port in Oza in Spain; you will love it!"

Michelle rolled those green eyes at him but chuckled all the same to see Lasse so excited about life again. The doubt that he would ever take her along was dismissed by seeing him come alive with his plans.

"You've already planned all this out, Sir."

"Yes, in fact, there is a guy in the next marina who is selling his sailboat. His wife recently died of cancer and he no longer wants to sail without her."

"Somebody doesn't want to sail without his wife?! Incredible!" Michelle teased Lasse.

"I heard he has some kind of brain cancer himself and he just needs to sell his boat. Let's head over there in the morning to take a look at it. If it is a decent price, then we can sell Sixteen Tons or perhaps he would consider a trade."

"Okay whatever you want, Darling. We will make it happen." Michelle said tenderly and honestly, but wistfully longing for the day when Lasse would give up sailing and settle for the farm life with her.

Tiny drops of rain began to angrily pierce the sky as the storm moved closer. Michelle stood on the bow and watched the thick, black clouds roiling ominously from the west to the north. The clanging of the mast riggings grew more intense as the wind whipped her clothes against her body and her hair behind her. Lasse stood and took her hand; she kissed him and looked resignedly into his eyes. He was going to do this his way and she had to accept it. He was planning his next adventure and her part was support and to listen to his stories, make his food, and outfit his new boat with provisions. Fine. She would do anything for this man. He knew that.

The next morning, Lasse drove Michelle over to Green Cove Springs Marina to look at Jim Miller's 32 foot 1984 Morgan Sloop. It was a bit rough but in sailable condition.

"Oh, yeah, she has seen blue water. The wife and I used to sail to the Bahamas all the time in her. I'm asking $35,000 firm," Mr. Miller said.

"Well, she does look solid," Lasse replied, always seeming to acquiesce to salesmen while he managed to work his own price into the end deal.

"She looks like a disaster," Michelle muttered under her breath while checking out the tiny galley and the barren saloon area while the men chatted above. "Looks like someone stripped her bare," she continued murmuring to herself while listening to her husband work his magic on poor Mr. Miller. If Lasse wanted that boat, he'd have it at his price; that was for certain.

"Join us for a cup of coffee over on Sixteen Tons this afternoon around 2 and let's discuss this, Jim," Lasse invited. Michelle shoved her sunglasses back on in the brightness of the morning sun as she climbed back outside to the deck of the boat. Poor Mr. Miller;

Michelle knew Lasse was going to try to trade the beloved mistress, Sixteen Tons, for this Morgan.

Jim Miller came right at 2pm and climbed aboard the old lady stashed on the hard in an area overgrown with weeds and geckos. Lasse and Michelle listened to the man's sad story and although Lasse had his ways, Mr. Miller wanted $35,000 cash for his boat.

Michelle served fresh French-pressed coffee to the men and listened casually while they chatted. She had heard Lasse hundreds of times cajole people into things they didn't want to do. He could make it happen.

"Got any sugar?" Mr. Miller requested.

"No, we sure don't. I'm sorry, we don't use sugar or any sweetener in our coffee," Michelle explained.

"You need sugar?" Lasse asked. "I've got sugar."

"Lasse, that sugar is old and has dead ants in it."

"I don't mind a few dead ants," Mr. Miller assured, taking the sugar container and shaking sweet granules and dead ants into his coffee. He just scooped the dead little bodies away with his spoon.

Seriously? Michelle thought. This can't be real. And then Mr. Miller drank that dreadful brew!

Before Mr. Miller had walked across Tom Holland's shipyard Lasse was berating him. "He will never get $35,000 for that boat, it isn't worth $20,000. He is crazy and he won't end up selling it." Michelle listened patiently, agreeing with a vigorous nod of her head and a serious scowl to match Lasse's. She knew Lasse was pissed off because he couldn't get Mr. Miller to come down on his price, ridiculous as it was.

She opened up her laptop and searched for other sailboats that were for sale in northeast Florida. "Look!" she proclaimed excitedly.

"This one is only $24,000 and in much better condition. Oh, Lasse, there are several for sale. You don't have to settle for that one boat. And here is your favorite, a Finnish made Nauticat! It is $68,000 but it is beautiful!"

"Let me see that," Lasse said, turning the laptop his way. His mind began to calculate how he could afford that boat. Michelle was going to need a well paying full-time career. They both looked at all the photos posted online and oohed and awed over the details and features of the motor sailor.

"A motor sailor would take us all over the world, Bambina." Lasse began to dream of traveling across the Atlantic. They could go to the Bahamas, Michelle could handle a one day trip like that.

"This is the kind of boat that would take us through the Panama Canal," Lasse said pensively. All of his life he had loved sailing and he was grateful to be well enough to get back at it. Michelle told him she would do whatever was necessary to help him make it happen. But he closed the laptop and told her that boat was too expensive. The afternoon was hot and humid; the air conditioning on board of Sixteen Tons was cranking out the cold air as best as it could.

"Let's head to Monkey Fist to look at a piece of teak I need to make a small mug rack. I'm going to hang it right here. What do you think, Baby?" Lasse asked holding up his hands to the port side of the helm where the galley was located.

"Let's go, Lover," she said, scooping up Daisy and heading for the door. They found what they needed at the local marine trading post but then Michelle saw a beautiful wooden boat being worked on in the shipyard. She happened to love the scrolling woodwork that was part of wooden boats. Lasse liked the practicality of fiberglass.

"No, Bambina, not that one," he stated firmly as he steered her away from it.

"But it is so beautiful, much more beautiful than that old, rotten Morgan!" Lasse never listened to her dreamy requests; the girl was a hopeless romantic. As if he wasn't. They both silently admired that big wooden sailboat and the man working on her repairs stopped and asked, "You folks interested in the boat?"

"No!"

"Yes!" Lasse and Michelle answered simultaneously. The man gave them the broker/owner's business card and Michelle managed to get Lasse to allow her to call him. The man was actually on the shipyard premises and met them immediately. After a short discussion, Michelle was grinning ear to ear.

"Lover! You can afford that boat! And look at how the repairs are being made so thoroughly! That is an ocean-going vessel if ever I saw one!"

"No, Bambina, that is not the one. We are going to have fiberglass only as it requires the least maintenance. I will keep the man's card in case we do need to call him in the future, though."

Michelle found it a joy to share in Lasse's dreams and to see him clear-minded and having wonderful plans for the next few years. Her efforts this afternoon were only to help Lasse purchase a better boat than that Morgan. Well, he wasn't crossing the Atlantic just yet; he still had to get Sixteen Tons back in the water. She contemplated how she could help him further while they drove back to Sixteen Tons with the car windows down, enjoying the hot sunshiny, early spring day, wind blowing throughout the car and palm branches waving peacefully. She would head home in the morning and try to figure something out.

Once back home she researched different boats and the trip across the Atlantic itself. She came across the autobiography, "Around the World in 80 Years," by Harry Heckel, Jr. That man had been eighty years old when he crossed the Atlantic. What a story, including his adventures on the Azores Islands. She bought the book and mailed it to Lasse in Green Cove Springs. It was just the thing to put the wind in the sails of his dreams.

Each morning Lasse would walk forty-five minutes around Reynolds Yacht Park and Tom Holland's shipyard, extending his path to include the junkyard of scrap metal that included many military refuse items such as a rusted out rocket fuel tank. The crunch of the gravel under his feet was keeping time with his military marching stride as he heard a car approaching behind him. He stepped off the gravel road and into the stiff and sharp weeds to wait for it to pass. The car sped passed him and stopped abruptly causing quite a little cloud of dust to fill the air around it. Then the car turned around and headed slowly towards Lasse. It was a little old lady driving right up to him. She put her window down and inquired, "Excuse me, Sir, do you know where the Beulah Baptist Church is located?"

"I am sorry, Ma'am," Lasse replied in his deep, charming British-English accent, his blue eyes twinkling, "I am not from around here."

"No, I can hear that you are not; where are you from?"

"Currently I am from Ohio but originally I am from Finland."

Then the most amazing thing happened. That little old lady in the middle of nowhere Florida began to speak in Finnish to Lasse. She said her parents had immigrated to the United States and although she was born in the USA, her parents had spoken Finnish in their home.

"What are you doing in this place if you are from Ohio?"

"I got cancer when I was cruising my boat the second time around the American Great Loop and I kind of became stuck here."

"Where is your wife? Doesn't she boat with you? Why are you alone?"

"My wife is in Ohio and she is unable to boat. She nearly empties the contents of her stomach just sitting on the boat in the harbor. But she would be with me if she could," he explained while using body language to show how Michelle always became nauseated on the boat.

"Sir, is Jesus Christ your Lord and Savior?" Sherry Turner got right to the point.

"Yes, He is!" Lasse zealously declared.

"May I pray with you?"

"Absolutely." Lasse was awed by the request.

And Sherry Turner got out of her car, took Lasse by the hands, and prayed over him. She asked the Lord to heal him, prayed that his cancer would not return, and that his wife would be able to boat with him. Lasse was overwhelmed. No one had ever taken his hands and prayed a prayer like that over him. God sent an angel to speak in Finnish to him in the forsaken old shipyard and then to pray healing over him. It was too incredible. He couldn't wait to call Michelle to tell her of this miracle that God had afforded him.

Michelle was amazed and thrilled that this impossible situation had happened to Lasse. She was ecstatic.

"Lasse! There is no way that some little old lady could find herself back behind Tom Holland's junkyard, find you, speak in Finnish, and pray healing over you! I am sure she was an angel sent by God!"

"And she was speaking in Finnish! I could not believe my ears!"

Their excitement stemmed from their faith that God certainly did intend healing for Lasse. But neither of them knew how desperate that battle was going to become, sooner rather than later.

"Lover, if it is God's will for me to boat with you, I will do it!"

Lasse chuckled and agreed that if God wanted her to boat and she didn't get sick when the boat was finally back on the water, then that is exactly what they would do. They were both filled with peace and happy tranquility.

In early May Michelle was serving as a test proctor for high schoolers at Dayton Christian. Her phone was on silent but she saw that she had received two missed calls from Lasse. Immediately she worried. She sent him a text that she was unable to call and asked if he was okay. He text back that Tom Holland was kicking him out of the boatyard so that he could rent the boat's space to another, more costly boat to whom he could charge twice the rent. Lasse was annoyed and worried about what to do but God was giving him just the push he needed to get back to boating.

Lasse went to bargain with Tom Holland but came across one of his shipyard employees instead. Lasse explained that he still had yet to repaint Sixteen Tons' bottom and he couldn't get her in the water until he had done that. He had spent all spring sanding and adding more fiberglass and she just was not ready to launch. The young man told Lasse to just hold on and that he would talk to Tom. Fifteen minutes later he returned and asked Lasse, "Do you want the good news or the bad news first?"

"Good, please," Lasse replied solemnly.

"The good news is that Tom Holland's sons are going to paint the bottom of your boat for free. The bad news is you owe me a six pack of beer."

Lasse was overjoyed and held his hands up to thank God and then shook the young man's hand boisterously. He was so grateful. He had waited two years to return to boating and God was kicking him out of this boatyard with a free paint job. He could not believe that God would bless him in such a way. He was humbled and grateful. Michelle cried when she heard how it had all worked out.

"Oh, Lover, God is certainly too good to us. You're going to be okay and now you will get back to your boating life."

And so, at dawn on the warm and breezy morning of May 12, 2017 Michelle filmed Lasse starting the engine of Sixteen Tons and making his way out of the St. John's River. That video represented the victory for life, and love, and the pursuit of Lasse's boating happiness. He raised his Finnish flag and then he raised his American flag and freedom coursed through his veins once more with the rumble of the 120 horse power Ford Lehman engine beneath him. Michelle waved goodbye once again from the shore but had to jump in the car with Daisy and get to the bridge where Lasse wanted to wave to her from the first moments of his next journey. He was the hopeless romantic. Michelle's pirate husband was sailing once more and cancer-free. She couldn't be more grateful.

Lasse called seven times a day once again as he was out on the Intracoastal Waterways along the East Coast and Michelle couldn't wait to hear his voice. Their spring had come and the winter was past, all the gloom of cancer was behind them. They made plans to host all the Finnish family in their home that summer.

"First Vivian and Viveka will come to stay for two weeks. We will pick them up in Washington D.C. and drop them back off there. Jere and his family will come the same day to Washington D.C. and we will drive back home to Brookville for one week then stay at Olverson's Lodge Creek vintage farm house. I have it all worked out, Bambina!"

"Lover, you used to give me at least twenty-four hours in between guests so I could get the house cleaned and fresh sheets on the beds! Now I have no time to do that! What day will they arrive?" Michelle asked excitedly.

It had been two years since she had seen all the girls and now they would all be there. Happy family life as it had been before was back in full swing. All the arrangements were made and Michelle was busy with meal and event planning; there would of course be family cookouts with corn hole tournaments. Those corn hole tournaments were a big deal between the American and Finnish family members. They'd had so much fun in years past and had so many great memories yet to make.

Lasse had made his way up the Intracoastal Waterway to Olverson's Marina on Lodge Creek, just out of the mouth of the Potomac River. He was back and he could not have been more satisfied and grateful. He said a prayer of thanks to God repeatedly as he cruised Sixteen Tons, the smell of the Atlantic and diesel combined to complete his life. He had crossed the Chesapeake Bay once again and this time she wasn't as rude as she had been when he headed south two years earlier through a severe storm.

It was the end of May and he was heading back home for a quick visit with Dr. John Brown for an MRI and bloodwork and to get a few minor house projects done before the visits began in a few weeks. Lasse and Michelle saw Dr. Brown for a brief visit and as soon as his blood was taken and the MRI complete, Lasse was back in the car and heading towards Sixteen Tons. He had no worries and neither did Michelle.

Dr. Brown called Michelle around 9pm the next night. Right away her fear radar went off; there was no reason for him to call at night unless he had bad news.

"Mr. Paivola has a small pearl-like something in his right lung. Now it may be nothing but I think we better investigate. Please have him come in to see me this week and we will get him scheduled for a biopsy."

Michelle called Lasse. They were both upset, confused, and borderline devastated.

"What kind of pearl is he talking about? As big as a pearl? What?" Lasse demanded.

"I don't know, Lover. All I know is that it was pearl-like. I don't know if that is a description of some kind of lung cancer or the size or shape; I don't know. And Dr. Brown didn't even sound sober."

"Shit. I will get things settled on the boat, pack up, and come home in two days."

"Okay. He said your appointment would be at the end of this week. Oh, Lasse, I am so sorry."

Before the biopsy another MRI was done, as well as a CT Scan. There were now five nodules, one small questionable place in the left lung and the other four in the right lung, one being the size of a pearl.

Lasse's CEA continued to rise and Michelle had a knot in the pit of her stomach. Fear. She heard God whisper, "Do you trust Me?"

Her honest and immediate reply was, "No." She was scared to death. There was no way she was going to live on this planet without Lasse.

The biopsy was done at the best hospital in the Dayton area and went very smoothly. A nurse had prayed with Lasse and Michelle and her words, "And Heavenly Father, we know You are the real Captain of this ship," struck a sweet spot in their hearts.

The results were malignant. They were both devastated but Lasse would not be beaten, that was for certain.

They met with Dr. Dick Hansen, who seemed very odd to Michelle, but he assured them that he would take a very small slice of Lasse's right lung that would remove four of these five nodules. Again the Da Vinci robot would be used for surgery. What the fuck, really? Michelle was angry that once again her husband would be subjected to a surgeon practicing his robotic skills. Lasse agreed to all of it and Michelle shook her head and disagreed. But he was the one man she didn't boss. She had never won an argument with Lasse, not even to save his life.

The surgery was scheduled for the first week of August. They had June and July to spend with all the family, Finnish and American. It was important that their family spend precious moments in love and to cherish each other. Lasse didn't want to upset any of them but to enjoy the time they had together.

Vivian and Viveka came and there were long chats with both Lasse and Michelle. Those weeks were filled with tears and hugs and prayers and kisses. Christopher, Marah, and Ivan shared their days with the girls; Vivian and Ivan hugging tightly in the close bond they shared. Ivan had been a toddler when Vivian would come and spend her summers with Michelle. He thought her home was here and that she must come back at any time because he missed her so much.

Marah took the girls to Vacation Bible School and spent lots of afternoons in the kitchen with them. They laughed and fought and baked homemade brownies and made videos together.

Michelle insisted that Lasse let Vivian drive his car because in America she would be getting her license at her age. He finally agreed, and buckled up, while Viveka and Michelle strapped themselves in the back seat, laughing the whole time. Vivian squealed the tires and turned too sharply and shouted that she didn't understand while Lasse shouted for her to go more slowly and turn less sharply. It was wonderful and unforgettable.

They hugged and cried goodbye at the Dulles International Airport, promising to see each other the following summer. Then Lasse and Michelle waited a couple of hours before Jere and his family arrived.

Both of them waited excitedly for the first sight of Jere and his gals. Lasse hugged Jere and Michelle hugged Jere's wife, Hanna, swapping and hugging their daughters, Ira and Ria. When Michelle hugged Jere she started to sob. Oh God, she prayed, can Jere help save Lasse? Please, Jere, help us. She was overcome with fear and emotion.

"Oh, Michelle," Jere said, as she excused herself to the nearby ladies' room. Pull yourself together, Michelle thought; they don't understand how bad this is and Lasse does not want them to be upset.

They drove through the Appalachian Mountains with all the ladies catching up for the years they had not seen each other. Lasse drove and Jere rode shotgun, both of them talking non-stop. The week with the family passed too quickly, family dinners, corn hole tournaments, and roller coasters at the local amusement park. Not much talk of cancer or the upcoming surgery had transpired. There were no empty words given that everything would be alright but there were hugs and smiles as they went through the departure gate at Dulles.

# CHAPTER SIXTEEN

The August morning of the surgery to remove part of Lasse's lung they prayed together and Michelle stood by Lasse's hospital bed waiting on Dr. Hansen. He was late. The nurses called to see if he was coming and the situation seemed disconcerting to Michelle. But Dr. Hansen finally arrived, unhurried and confident. He assured Michelle that he would take care of Lasse when she told him, "After God, Lasse is most important to me."

Everything seemed okay as Lasse woke from the surgery. He had an epidural in his back and a drain from the incision. Their nurse, Erica, was incredible. She loved hearing their story and laughed with them when Michelle recounted, "In Finland you would get a ticket for that!"

"I thought she married me for love, but no, it was for revenge!" Lasse said.

"Oh, I don't believe that!" Erica stated, laughingly. "You guys are the most amazing couple I have ever worked with. I want to hear more tomorrow before I remove your drain!"

Lasse sat in the chair with his iPad and tapped his foot to Little Richard's, "Long Tall Sally", declaring he was going to get them thrown out of the hospital for his loud rock and roll. Michelle took a video of him and shook her head, beaming. He was okay. "Thank You, God," she whispered continually.

Lasse was worried that he hadn't been given his Imodium because he was not able to move from the bed very quickly. It had been more than a year since his reversal and he knew his body would send him to the toilet six times a day. Erica assured him everything would be okay and if he felt he needed that Imodium she would make sure he received it. He never needed Imodium another day in his life. The robotic surgery had damaged his upper bowel and he had lost all motility. And a new nightmare began.

The first of September Lasse declared himself well enough to go back to his boat. Michelle had a few days free and although she wanted to spend Lasse's birthday with him, she refused to go to Olverson's Marina just to sit aboard Sixteen Tons. She invited Lasse to join her on the beach at Emerald Isle. Stubborn, they each spent that weekend apart. It was good for Michelle to be alone on the beach and cry out all her lost frustrations to God. He always listened. Sometimes she could hear back from Him. She was pissed off that once again, Lasse chose to be on his boat instead of with her. She wanted to live every day with the man whom her soul loved. He needed his mistress, Sixteen Tons, to hide on and just try to survive. He didn't have the strength to walk the beach, hand and hand with Michelle. But he didn't tell her that. She returned from her beach weekend revived and holding God's hand. She loved her pirate husband even if he was always leaving her behind. She prayed for answers to help Lasse's healing from this surgery.

Lasse was in a lot of pain but refused anything stronger than Tylenol. He tried to work on Sixteen Tons but the pain was more than he could handle. This was a man who had been shot twice, stabbed multiple times, and beaten with a baseball bat. He knew pain. He drove home and asked Michelle to get him in to see the lung surgeon, Dr. Hansen, for the pain.

Michelle called Dr. Hansen's office three times and left three messages about all the pain Lasse was living with before the doctor reluctantly returned her calls. She was pissed off.

"Dr. Hansen is an ignorant ass! And I am tired of him ignoring us!" Michelle ranted to Lasse. Her emotions were out of control to see him suffering like this.

When they were finally offered an appointment with Dr. Hansen, he told Lasse that the strange lump he had on his right side and all the pain was just some fluid or air that would eventually dissolve into his tissues. He just needed to be more patient.

"This man has been shot twice, Dr. Hansen, he knows what pain is and if he is telling you something isn't right then you need to figure out what is wrong." Michelle demanded.

Dr. Hansen looked like he himself was sick and just finished a round of chemotherapy. If he did care, he didn't show it.

"I know my body and this lump is like an alien," Lasse tried to explain. "And I am no longer going to the toilet six times a day, something isn't right."

"Well, it sounds like that problem has been solved," Dr. Hansen replied.

Michelle was livid. "So, you're saying that there is no block-age, nothing is wrong, the previous excessive bowel movements are solved, and the pain and bulging is just from excess fluid or air from the surgery?" She didn't believe his bullshit.

"Mr. Paivola, I can give you a steroid shot that will help the pain for five or six weeks, do you want that?"

"No, I don't want to mask the pain; I want to know what is causing it."

"Well, there's nothing else I can do to help you then. You can continue to take Tylenol for the pain."

With that, they were dismissed. Angry and frustrated they drove home. The radio was on and an ad for an attorney who handles injury lawsuits came on, offering that you could call "the tiger" if you needed. Lasse said, "I'm calling the tiger. This is ridiculous."

Michelle was filled with anger and frustration but she didn't have time to deal with it. She had to find answers for Lasse. She called Dr. Turner, Lasse's family doctor. He agreed that something was not right and perhaps they had better test his gall bladder and liver. She called Dr. Brown and he was quite unhappy with the news. He called Michelle back and told her to take Lasse to the emergency room as he was worried that it could be his gall bladder and that Lasse was having gall bladder attacks. Michelle believed that this was again another cover up of faulty medicine.

Lasse remained calm and endured the pain. Michelle admired him. He was just the best. He was brave. She was not brave. He was quiet while she raved. He was strong and she was tearful.

The emergency room was packed when Michelle took Lasse in, according to Dr. Brown's instructions. Lasse was put on a gurney out in the hall and he wanted to disappear for a few minutes in blissful sleep. He had a habit of covering his face when sleeping publically but Michelle insisted he remove the sheet from his head as he was scaring the other ER patients. They both chuckled.

Lasse was taken back for a quick CT scan and x-ray. A young emergency room doctor, Dr. Todd Jones, came to sit with Michelle and to prepare her to hear the worst news. "This could be liver cancer, Mrs. Paivola. We don't know yet, but I just want you to be aware that this might be very serious."

Michelle nodded and thanked him. He is just a kid, she thought. Dear God, help me to be strong for Lasse, she prayed.

After Dr. Jones and the intern examined all of the information the intern declared, "Old man, you're full of crap! Your upper bowel has been damaged and is paralyzed so you don't have peristalsis, those natural ocean-like waves your intestines use to pass stool aren't working. All you need are two Senokot and that will fix you."

"Two Senokot? He is used to taking six Imodium every day. Are you sure?" Michelle asked, so grateful they hadn't said it was liver cancer.

"Yep, you can see all this on the x-ray, that's a whole lot of crap in there. Keep it moving with two Senokot in the morning and two at night and he will be fine."

Lasse was in constant pain. In mid-November he drove back to the marina in Virginia to winterize Sixteen Tons. He had hoped to stay a few days but was so miserable that he completed the work and came right back home.

"Bambina, something is so wrong. Not even this Senokot is helping and this alien inside me is getting bigger."

Michelle sighed heavily. "Lover, I do not know what else to do. I don't know who to call. Do you want me to call Dr. Brown?"

"We will see him in a few days, just wait." Lasse was suffering terribly but quietly.

"Let me call him, Lasse. Let's just let him know how you're feeling and see what he says. Okay?"

"Okay."

On November 16, 2017 Lasse was admitted to the hospital. A few days later Lasse had an endoscopy done by Dr. Murphy. Dr. Murphy was very kind and as Lasse was in recovery he sat directly across from Michelle and gave her his honest opinion.

"Mrs. Paivola, I placed two stents in your husband's bile ducts." He took out a piece of paper and pen and drew out the gall bladder, liver, and the ducts that connect the two.

"I saw something in one of his ducts, a blockage that may be a tumor. He may have cancer, liver cancer."

Michelle took a long slow breath, "Well, we have heard those words before. We will deal with it." She held it together but it was a miracle. Her mind was racing. What the fuck? Liver cancer? Everyone dies with liver cancer. He is not going to die. He is not.

"Thank you, Dr. Murphy." Michelle rose from her seat in the waiting area as Lasse was being wheeled down the hall on a hospital bed. She walked quickly towards him as he was being taken back to his room.

"Lover, you're okay." She brushed his cheek with her fingers and looked into his glazed eyes.

"It hurts."

"I know. I'm sorry, Lasse. You should begin to feel a little bit better soon, my love."

The next day they headed home and Michelle cared for Lasse tenderly. Thanksgiving was in four days. Lasse handled the liver cancer news bravely. How could he be so brave? Michelle was devastated.

They met with Dr. Brown on Wednesday before Thanksgiving and he entered the room with the words, "I'm sorry." Fucking be sorry, Michelle thought; he is not going to die.

"Let's schedule a PET scan next week and I will research which chemotherapy protocol to follow. We will see exactly what we are dealing with and begin the fight."

"Thank you, Dr. Brown," Lasse said. They left his office holding hands, fingers interlocked. This was not good.

"Hey, let's go to Dorothy Lane Market and split a sandwich for our date!" Michelle suggested. They had visited the area's only gourmet grocery store many times in the past after doctor visits.

"Let's do it," Lasse said worriedly.

When they returned home, Lasse planted himself on the couch with their tiny dog, Daisy, and Michelle got started preparing dishes for the next day's Thanksgiving dinner with the family.

Michelle knew the recipes by heart and began chopping onions, celery, fresh sage, and apples for the dressing she served annually. It was one of her favorites even though only she and Lasse liked it. She made a box of Stovetop Stuffing for everyone else.

Her mind went down several avenues trying to solve Lasse's cancer. What about this? What about that? And, what if? No, that what if was not going to be their outcome. But Steve Jobs. Yeah, what about Steve Jobs? All his money couldn't cure his liver cancer. Hot, angry, helpless tears slid down her cheeks as she stirred in the broth, melted butter, cream, and cognac. She sniffled a few times but kept her misery to herself in the kitchen.

Lasse heard her and came into the kitchen. He hugged her and then taking her by the arms and looking into her eyes said, "Bambina, where is your faith? I am going to walk through this. I do not care who has not made it through this, then I will be the first!"

Michelle believed him with all her heart and held him tightly to her. There was no other acceptable outcome. He would live. That's the deal. That had been their sauna deal when he was first diagnosed with colon cancer two and a half years ago. He lives. That's it. She smiled at him through her tears and said, "Okay."

Lasse handed Michelle his iPad and she thought he must have found some new, cutting edge cure for liver cancer. She clicked the YouTube video he had pulled up and it was a raunchy prostitute song, "Don't Cry for Louie"! She cracked up when the singer belted out, "Don't cry for Louie, Louie wouldn't cry for you!"

"Oh, Lasse! You wouldn't cry for me, for sure!"

"I will make it, Bambina, so have some faith." He smiled at her, bolstering her spirit.

"You have to make it. You're irreplaceable. I love you and I could never make it without you."

"I love you, Bambina, I will make it, I promise," he answered as he hugged her. Whatever was going to happen, he prayed to make it until her birthday in February. Since the stubborn woman had never allowed him to get life insurance all he had to take care of her was his Finnish pension. If she was fifty years old before he died then she would get part of that for the rest of her life and it would be enough to help her survive. He prayed, "God, let me live until she is fifty and ten seconds old."

Two weeks later, Lasse's pain had not relented. He hurt and told his doctors about his growing "alien". They just kind of shook their heads and said it was still fluid or trapped air from the lung surgery. No one had answers except to offer him the steroid shot for pain. He continued to refuse it because he needed to know there was pain in order for them to find the reason. None of them had another solution. And then the fevers began.

"Bambina, is it cold in here?" Lasse asked Michelle, trembling. He was on the couch and hugging himself.

"Lover, no, it's not. Do you have a fever?" He was a bit warm, she noted as she ran her hand across his forehead, cheeks, and neck. "Let me get the thermometer."

When she returned thirty seconds later, Lasse's trembling was bordering uncontrollable. Holy shit, she thought.

His temperature was 100.3°F; not enough to be alarmed about or to call the doctor on call just yet. Lasse begged her to cover him with quilts and the heating pad, which she did. Whenever her sons had fevers, she kept them lightly covered and rubbed their skin with cool washcloths. But she instinctively agreed with Lasse that he needed to be covered. She sat down on the floor beside the couch and put her hand on top of his quilts. She prayed silently over him and dread filled her soul; she was frozen with fear. This could only be a very bad sign.

Michelle called Dr. Turner, the family doctor, and took Lasse to see him. He agreed that none of this was a good sign and to keep a close eye on Lasse's fevers. Dr. Turner was studying Lasse's online charts continuously and told them to call him if needed. He just didn't have any answers. It exasperated Michelle that no one seemed to be able to help. Did any of them know what to do? Was this what "practice" meant in the medical field?

Michelle whispered prayers over Lasse constantly and she put frankincense on his swelling abdomen every night. Lasse began asking her to get the "Frankenstein" and to put it on him. Somehow it was a comfort and the smell was unique and clean. Lasse couldn't handle getting in and out of the bed because of his pain and so Michelle made his bed on the couch. She closed the curtains and adjusted them so that no bit of light came through from the street to disturb Lasse's sleep.

As the days grew colder in December she began hand-sewing red linen sheets for him. She had read that real linen could have a healing effect on the body and she would try anything at this point. As soon as he was healed, the red sheets would be perfect for his bunk on Sixteen Tons.

On December 10th Michelle headed to Cleveland for the day with her sisters and Michael came to stay with Lasse. She had prepared a roasted chicken for the men and Michael served it. They had the sweetest visit together and later Lasse assured Michelle that Michael was doing just fine. When Michelle got home from the day trip that evening she sat in the big leather chair across from Lasse, who was wrapped in blankets on the couch. He listened intently to her story, offered advice, and trembled with chills.

"Lover, do you want me to take you to the hospital? What could be wrong?"

"I don't know yet. Let's see if this passes."

But the trembling grew worse. Michelle's fear turned to anger and frustration. Why couldn't something go right to help Lasse? Lasse reached for her hand and she knelt on the floor next to him. Very quickly Lasse's breathing turned to heavy panting and his body began to convulse. She dialed the on-call oncologist who told her to take Lasse to the emergency room. The episode had lasted nearly twenty minutes and as soon as she could she helped him into the car and drove him to the ER.

The emergency room doctor said, "He has an infection, sepsis, but we're not sure which strain. This most likely came with the stent placement. These convulsions are called rigors and it is the body's way of fighting the infection." Lasse was admitted to the hospital and as he stood up out of the wheelchair to get into the bed he began to convulse again. Michelle had to lay across his legs to keep them from flying off the hospital bed. When the fever seizure passed, she undressed Lasse and helped him into a gown, asking the nurse aide for several heated blankets.

Lasse was also jaundiced and had turned yellow. His stool was pale grey and his urine looked like dark tea. Michelle was terrified and functioned on auto-pilot. She made sure every new doctor, intern, nurse, and nurse aide knew that Lasse was a 15,000 steps a day FitBit guy and he had just been sailing a boat on the Atlantic a couple of months ago.

Lasse held Michelle's hand as she slept in a recliner beside his bed. Shit, this was not going well. His thoughts repeatedly worked through how to fight this but his prayers were constant, "Heavenly Father, let me live until she is fifty years old." Her birthday was just two months away. February 14th was his goal for living; any time beyond that was just bonus. As bad as Lasse felt, he knew it would take every bit of his strength to make it two more months. Lasse knew Michelle was a fighter, a survivor; she would make it no matter what happened. The reality that he might not have much longer to live really sunk in. He'd fight; he just didn't know if he'd win.

Michelle slept in the recliner for several nights and then a fold out cot was brought to Lasse's room. The nurses recognized her devotion to Lasse and that she wasn't leaving his side. She still emptied every bed pan and urinal, and she bathed him tenderly, changing his sheets herself making sure he was clean and as comfortable as possible. She massaged his legs and body, making sure he wore the massage boots in the bed to prevent blood clots. She took notes of every doctor's visit and looked up medical terms she didn't know to explain to Lasse what was said. What else could she do but pray? When the rigors came time after time while Lasse's body battled the sepsis infection, the nurses closed the door while Michelle laid her body across his to keep him in the bed. Why did the hospital staff leave them alone to deal with this? Was there nothing they could do to help?

Michael, Christopher, Marah, and Ivan all came to see Lasse. They brought salads and snacks and coffee and hugs. They stayed in that room just to be near Lasse so he could feel their love. Ivan brought a book, "Eat and Heal." He insisted, "Granny, this book says if you eat certain vegetables you can heal cancer. We've got to get those vegetables into Poppi right now!"

"Ivan, that is correct; eating the right foods helps to fight cancer but it is meant to prevent cancer. Poppi eats all those things and as soon as he is feeling a little better, we will make sure he keeps eating them. Thank you for loving your Poppi so much, Ivan!" Michelle hugged their grandson tightly, holding on to him as he held on to his faith.

Ivan continued, "Granny, I know Poppi will get better because I am praying for him. I got down on my knees in my bedroom and I sang "This Fragile Breath" to God and then I raised my hands and prayed, 'God! If you have to shake the whole earth to heal my Poppi, please do it!'"

Michelle was so blessed by Ivan and his faithful, loyal, fierce love for Lasse. She believed that little boy's prayers were heard and answered by God Almighty.

They were continually offered chaplains to come in and speak with them until finally Lasse, holding Michelle's hand, said, "She's my chaplain."

Michelle replied, "And he's mine." They had prayed together and spoke of all things heavenly. There was no need to bring in some-one who could not understand the depth of the faith they shared and they didn't want to feel obligated to explain to someone who didn't know them.

Dr. Bartholomew was the gastrointestinal surgeon who replaced Lasse's bile duct stents three times in one week as they kept filling up with puss. He concluded that yes, there was infection, but that did not necessarily mean there was more cancer. The infection could also cause a bounce in the CEA levels so he said not to panic but to wait patiently while the infection was clearing. Both Lasse and Michelle thanked God for this good man. The hospitalist doctors didn't seem to have a clue what was going on with Lasse's body and they offered no hope. With the hospitalists came a crowd of eager internists whose guesses left little hope to hang on to; their words brought only despair and unnecessary worry. Michelle continued to explain that the scrawny, jaundiced man they saw in the hospi-tal bed was not her husband; that Lasse was a fit man sailing a boat just a couple of months ago. They didn't even bother to listen but rather drew their own conclusions. They began to speak words of death over Lasse. He became discouraged and Michelle became livid. Dr. Bartholomew understood them and his diagnosis was completely hopeful.

Dr. Patel, the infectious disease doctor, was also a God-send. He was completely confident that Lasse would recover from the infection and be able to successfully conquer his cancer battle. He came to sit with Lasse and got to know both him and Michelle, assuring them that Lasse needed to strengthen his body. He suggested Michelle get Orgain, a good brand of protein to add to Lasse's non-existent diet, and told Lasse that even getting up to the chair in the room would build his strength. Lasse trusted in Dr. Patel's encouragement and gained hope enough to keep trying.

The hospitalist oncologists gave conflicting information and they never agreed with the outside doctors. Dr. Ahmed told Lasse that once his bile ducts were opened with the stents, the liver would clear the infection. Lasse asked, "Why do all the doctors say the stents were the source of infection but the surgeon says it was the pockets of pus and abscesses in the liver, not the stents? I do not understand." There was a question that possibly the lung surgery months earlier had damaged Lasse's liver and that was the reason he had swelling and infection. The doctors continued guessing and issuing their own opinions but no one agreed. Michelle took notes and tried to sort out all the information. One team seemed to think Lasse would recover and be fine and the other team seemed to think this was the end of Lasse's life. They chose to believe the team who pushed for longer life.

It was all of two weeks before Lasse's jaundice color subsided and the IV antibiotics began to kill the sepsis infection. His urine returned to a golden yellow instead of the tea color and he was released from the hospital. It was December 23, 2017. He would need IV antibiotics to continue for weeks at home and a hospitalist social worker came to discuss options with them.

"These IV drugs cost thousands of dollars and we want you to clearly understand your options, Mr. Paivola. If you choose to enter a rehab, there is the possibility that they will pay for your medicine and you would get free care."

"What's a rehab?" Michelle asked intently, taking notes.

"A nursing home," the young social worker stated.

"What? A nursing home?" Michelle asked incredulously. "Hell, no, my husband isn't going into any nursing home! I will sell my car, sell my house before he ever goes to a nursing home!" Michelle's tone and the volume of her voice shocked the social worker, who gasped, and replied,

"Well, these drugs may be thousands and thousands of dollars!"

"I do not care! My husband will never go to a nursing home!"

Lasse grinned as the social worker turned on her heel, long hair trailing behind her, and high-tailed it out of his room. "Oh, Bambina, you told her!"

"And I mean it, too, Lasse! Whatever it costs to get you better does not matter! What a racket! Oh my gosh, the nursing home will pay for your drugs to get you to stay there. They bill your insurance and eat the cost of the medicine because they will over charge for their very poor medical care." Michelle was livid. Her fight instinct was never disengaged these days and she was always tense. Like hell would she ever let one of those nasty places take over her husband's care. Only horror stories came out of the local nursing home. She would sell the car and the house if it came to that. Dear God, please send help; that was her constant prayer. Who could they believe?

Once again Lasse was tucked into his temporary bed on the sofa in the living room and Michelle began to chart his weight, blood pressure, temperature, and all output. At 9:00 a.m. a home health nurse would arrive for the first IV infusion at home.

The doorbell rang and Michelle opened it to a familiar face.

"Hi, I am Bonnie Holbrook, I am Mr. Paivola's nurse this morning."

"Bonnie Holbrook? Did your son attend Dayton Christian School in the early 90's?" Michelle asked.

"Yes, he did."

"Is this his photo?" Michelle asked Bonnie as she opened her planner, revealing a picture of Michael and Christopher as young boys, eating a picnic lunch in a tree alongside Bonnie's son.

"Wow; that is my son. How incredible that God would arrange this meeting."

Bonnie was amazing and another sign that God was for Lasse and for more life for Lasse. When she finished administering his IV antibiotics she asked Lasse if she could pray for him. It was the most faith-filled, beautiful, healing prayer they could have hoped to hear. That dear, Godly woman prayed that all of Lasse's organs would heal and begin to function as God intended and that his cancer would begin to go away and that he would be completely healed. The three of them held hands as Bonnie prayed and the faith was thick, stronger than the death that was trying to claim Lasse. There were so many miracles like this one. Bonnie hugged both of them and she told Lasse, "Do not do anything these doctors tell you unless you hear from God. You listen in your spirit and do what He tells you."

The peace of God filled them and Lasse was able to rest and trust. Hours later the phone rang and it was the home health nurse reporting that she would be there in the late afternoon. Michelle told her that a home health nurse had already been there and administered the antibiotics and they didn't need her.

"What was that home health care nurse's name?" the woman demanded.

"It was Bonnie," Michelle replied.

"I am Bonnie! I am supposed to be your nurse for the day!"

"It was Bonnie Holbrook who was here already." But Michelle knew this little mix up was God's doing; he sent a praying, faith-filled nurse and not this grumpy nurse who would never have prayed healing over Lasse. Thank You, Heavenly Father, Michelle whispered. Thank You, Jesus.

Morning brought a different home health nurse, who evaluated Lasse's condition and said, "Sounds to me that somebody nicked your liver during that surgery and it finally caused an infection." That was accurate but what could be done at that point? The surgeon who performed that surgery said the lump and pain were strictly air and fluid that would eventually dissipate. He didn't give Lasse another thought but Michelle hoped and prayed he would suffer the same as he had caused. She was so deeply angry at all Lasse had suffered.

The last day of 2017 ended early for Lasse and Michelle. He had tried to eat as much as he could to gain strength and she had anointed him with frankincense, praying over him as she tucked him carefully into his temporary bed on the sofa. She closed the blinds and then the heavy drapes to block out all light from the street. She did this each night; anything that could make his life more comfortable was her goal. A fire was making its way out and cast only a dim, amber glow in the room. Lasse loved the fire and sleeping beside it brought him a sense of peace-filled calm. After many tiny good night kisses, Michelle looked down on Lasse from the end of the couch before going to bed. "Good night, Lover. God bless and keep you."

"Good night, Bambina," he whispered weakly, "God bless you, too."

"I love you, Lasse."

"I love you, too, Michelle."

The IV antibiotics were completed by January 10, 2018 and a visit to Dr. Patel was made to remove the PICC line. The doctor declared Lasse healed of the sepsis infection and encouraged him to build his strength and gain some weight.

The following day was a visit to a new doctor to discuss a colonoscopy and the status of Lasse's liver function and cancer in the liver and bile ducts. January 11th was bitterly cold and Michelle supported Lasse as she got him from the car and into the doctor's office. They chatted hopefully as flurries filled the stone colored sky and once again they determined they would win no matter who hadn't been able to beat cholangiocarcinoma.

The new female doctor came in and said, "Well, there's no need to conduct a colonoscopy because your prognosis isn't good."

Michelle was confused. "What?"

Lasse sat rigidly on the exam table, having only had his blood pressure and temperature taken. Fear cut into his soul and took up residence because of that doctor's words.

"What do you mean?" Michelle tried to clear her mind of this absolutely unacceptable statement.

"Mr. Paivola's prognosis isn't good. There is no need to do a colonoscopy."

"Ma'am, he's having rectal bleeding and we need to know why; he needs the colonoscopy to find the reason." Michelle was livid at the cold, hard facts and the emotionless delivery from this stranger.

"Well, I can give him one but there is no need to do one when his prognosis isn't good." If she said it one more time Michelle was going to blow up.

Lasse got off the table and said despairingly, "Let's go."

As they made their way back to the car, Lasse relied more on Michelle to help him than he wanted. He felt tired and so weak; this news was breaking him.

Michelle cussed and cursed and shouted. "That woman should not be a doctor! What kind of attitude is that? How dare she say that to us? She doesn't know us! She has no idea what is going on with you and she just says we should give up!" She was livid and terrified; she could hardly get the car out of the parking lot and back onto the busy Dayton street.

The flurries had only been the prologue to the snow storm that was now upon them. Michelle drove slowly through the white downpour and once in their driveway, jumped out of the car to help Lasse into the house and to the bathroom before she could pull the car into the garage. "Dear God, please," was her constant prayer as she helped Lasse undress, built a fire, and heated some homemade soup for her love. The storm outside was nothing compared to the storm inside Michelle. Rage built up in her soul and she just wanted to kill that doctor.

"Okay, Lasse, we need a better plan. We have to do what Dr. Patel said; get some weight on you and build your strength."

Lasse nodded slowly but he was so tired. His weight was the lowest ever in his adult life, 166 pounds. The lump and pain on his right side that came from the damage done during his lung surgery had not subsided, he had no appetite, and he had no strength. He silently prayed, "God, please let me live until she is fifty years old." He repeated this prayer over and over. He had a deep sense in his spirit that this was a downhill battle.

They made their way through the weekend with protein drinks and short walks around the inside of the house. Lasse was so weak that he would put his hand on Michelle's shoulder so he wouldn't lose his balance as they slowly made their rounds. She helped him to the bathroom and bathed him carefully in the shower. She tucked him into the linen sheets she had made for him and declared he would use them on the boat. She always had a word of hope and plans for a future. There was no way she was going to let words of doubt seep into their souls. To her, Lasse was irreplaceable and it was unacceptable to entertain the thought that he would not survive this battle. He would; of course he would. He must.

After Michelle washed Lasse's hair and towel-dried his body, she helped him get into his bathrobe. "Would you please dry my hair? I am so cold," he asked while trembling, sitting carefully on the closed lid of the toilet.

"Absolutely, Lover." And she began to brush his silvery-white hair back while using the blow dryer. Lasse looked deeply into Michelle's eyes while she worked the brush through his hair; he was so grateful for her limitless love and tender care. She would do anything for him and there was no way she could live without him. He was her life, he was her soul. It was a moment that wouldn't ever be forgotten and his message of gratitude was received without a word between them.

Michelle cringed at her efforts with Lasse's hair. Somehow she had created the dream coif of every elderly lady, full rolling and fluffy curls. He's going to kill me, she thought.

"There you go!" she said pleasantly and put the blow dryer away, hoping he wouldn't look in the mirror. She let him steady himself on her arms and yes, he did look in the mirror as they passed.

"Shit," he said as Michelle giggled and began to apologize.

"It will calm down overnight, Lasse, do not worry!" Their eyes met in the mirror and hers twinkled her adoration of this man who was her whole world. "Come on; let's get you into bed, Sir." He kept his hand on her shoulder all the way to the couch and she tenderly tucked him in.

"Don't forget the Frankenstein," Lasse reminded her.

"I won't forget," she replied as she grabbed the frankincense from the bathroom. She shook several drops onto her wrist and then carefully rubbed Lasse's belly with the essential oil. "The Lord bless you and keep you, Lasse. The Lord make His face shine upon you and give you His peace. The Lord heal you and forgive you."

"Amen," he sighed. He knew he was cherished and he knew God was taking care of him. His body hurt and he was exhausted but he had to keep up this fight until February 14th. "Until she is fifty, Lord."

On January 18, 2018 Lasse and Michelle met again with the oncologist, Dr. Brown. Michelle would later write in her journal, "Worst News of My Life". Lasse felt so weak as he waited for the doctor to come into the room that he put his head against the wall and fell asleep. They were not prepared to receive the news Dr. Brown delivered.

"I'm sorry," he said with a short pause. "Monday's CT scan shows multiple tumors in both lungs now."

He let that sink in for a very brief moment. Michelle was stone cold terrified and Lasse did not understand any of the doctor's words. He pulled up the scan on the large screen so they could see for themselves and began pointing with the tip of his pen.

"How many?" was all Michelle managed.

"There are about twenty-five tumors in the right lung and maybe a few more than that in the left lung; more than fifty in total. The CEA is at 71, the highest it has ever been." He wanted to get this over with as quickly as possible. He hated delivering bad news but it was a big part of the work he did.

Michelle nodded, "Okay. What do we do?"

Dr. Brown stated clinically, "We can start a new chemo within a couple of days and a new immunotherapy drug, but understand, we are not talking about years any longer; we are talking about months."

Michelle understood. Dear God. She clenched her jaw and steeled her nerves; she could freak out later. Although Lasse heard with his ears, his brain did not compute the message. He had not understood the doctor was telling him he only had a few months to live. Michelle understood but she did not accept it. She refused to accept this fatal diagnosis. She had always been fierce in her efforts to protect Lasse and she could not, she would not accept any outcome but life for him and with him. She would do whatever it took to move this mountain of cancer and death out of Lasse's path. She would shield him and carry him and feed him, whatever was necessary to keep him alive.

Michael, Christopher, Marah, and Ivan all came for a family dinner that Sunday. Michelle had told them the news immediately when they left the doctor's office and they understood how gravely ill Lasse was right now. But they also believed that prayer and the next chemotherapy could change this projected outcome. They laughed together and made the best of the dinner, drinking more wine than usual. Lasse assured them all once more, this family that loved him so dearly, "I don't care who hasn't walked through this, I will be the first!" And they all believed him wholeheartedly. He had to make it. If anyone could make it, Lasse could. He would.

The chemotherapy appointment was the following Wednesday, which was bitterly cold and dreary, but the crystal chandeliers all throughout the new cancer center sparkled anyway. Their mood was somber, resigned as they held hands walking through the pristine hallways that shown like a palace. Lasse was so weak and his bloodwork hadn't been what it needed to be in order to administer the drugs.

Dr. Brown came to the station where Lasse was seated in a reclining chair and said, "Mr. Paivola, you're not strong enough for the chemo so we're just gonna give you the immunotherapy drug, Vectibix alone. It's a start, not as good as giving the chemo, too, but we will do that next week." He rubbed Lasse's bony forearm as he spoke. Lasse just nodded, grateful to be reclining and ready to cover his face, close his eyes, and escape into sleep.

Their nurse, Louise, was the sweetest lady. She started the infusion and left them in their private cubicle. Michelle sat next to Lasse, praying silently. "Bambina, I am cold," Lasse said as he began to tremble. His eyes were wide as he looked to her for help and she knelt down beside him. In the next two minutes he was in a full-force rigors episode. Four nurses came, Dr. Brown came, and two nurse assistants came. Michelle told them they had been rushing the fever by piling on heated blankets and that is just what they did.

"There are two schools of thought on these fevers," Louise said. "Some people stop them with ice and others bring it on with heat. It seems that heat is the best for Lasse." All those around Lasse poured out love and concern for him.

A kind lady grabbed Michelle and hugged her. "I am praying for your husband. I am sorry you are both going through this but you know the Lord is with you. You know that right?" Was she an angel?

Michelle nodded as she wiped the tears away. Dear God, this suffering is unbearable, she thought.

Lasse's blood pressure was so low and this episode drained him of all his strength. He slept with exhaustion in the recliner as Michelle watched the Vectibix course through the infusion machine and into Lasse. He will be okay. He will live and not die in the Name of Jesus. She prayed it over and over and over. She practically carried Lasse into the house.

The last day of January 2018 Lasse had permanent bile duct stents placed by Dr. Bartholomew. As Lasse sat in the recovery room, Dr. Bartholomew came to chat. "Look, you can make it. These stents are permanent and you won't need anything more put in while you're getting chemo. Keep fighting. I'll be off for the next six months getting my wrists worked on – carpal tunnel," he stated, holding up his wrists. "There's nothing that says this cancer is going to kill you, Lasse, so you keep fighting. And I will see you when I get back from my own surgery. Take care." Dr. Bartholomew took a swallow of the Pepsi he had with him and then smiled kindly at them before walking towards the exit.

"Oh, Lover, I told you, you're going to be okay. Dr. Bartholomew knows this and like you said, we will walk through this!" Michelle was emotionally charged with the excitement and hope that whatever it took, Lasse was going to make it. Dr. Bartholomew believed that and so could they. "God bless that man! Jesus, thank You for Dr. Bartholomew."

The first week of February brought a funeral of the grandson of one of Michelle's best friends. The next day their good friend and neighbor died. Lasse was not able to attend the funerals, he was hardly holding onto life himself. But he did have something to look forward to; Jere and Lauri, his sons, were coming for a visit from Finland on February 17th. "Lord, please let me live to see Jere and Lauri. Jere and Lauri, Lord, let me see them once again please." He prayed for this fervently. Michelle busied herself with all things needed to prepare for their visit and with strengthening Lasse the best she could. She was hopeful and positive and looking forward to seeing Lasse's happiness to see Jere and Lauri. Jere would encourage Lasse; she trusted in him.

Marah planned a sweet family dinner for Michelle's fiftieth birthday. Lasse did not have the strength to attend; chemotherapy and mini-rigors continued and literally drained him of life. But Marah did send him a boxed homemade dinner and her homemade lemon raspberry cake which he gratefully managed to eat and even smiled as Michelle took his picture.

Michelle helped Lasse to shower and shave and once again dried his hair but kept the fluffy curls to a minimum this time. He sat on the toilet lid while she worked the brush and hot air through his hair. It had only thinned slightly with the chemo. "Your hair looks great, Lover," Michelle declared as he used her arms for support while rising. He had only the towel around his waist as he put his hands on her shoulders and they passed the bathroom mirror.

"Shit." His evaluation of how thin he looked. His cheekbones hung below his yellow eyes like craggy rocks protruding from a cliff, his cheeks sunken, and his pallor a yellowish grey. Each of his ribs was visible as his dehydrated skin sucked the marrow from his ribcage. He did look like a survivor from Auschwitz. What a horror.

"Yes, you are skinny, Lover," Michelle nodded as she acknowledged his true physical state, "but you're still sexy as ever!" And Michelle meant it. She was more in love with Lasse than she ever had been. Her love grew for him every day in all the moments they walked through this hell fire. Every torture drew them closer together, purified them of all that came before, and prepared them for what was to come.

Michelle helped Lasse as he put on his flannel lined jeans and the new Filson green plaid flannel shirt she had ordered for him. He would kill her if he found out she paid $125 for that shirt. It was the best quality and would last him for the next ten years was her justification. And she wanted to keep him warm. Her heart broke to see him cold or suffering and the least she could do was dress him warmly and snuggle him by the fires she kept going. He was worth it.

Michelle helped Lasse into the car and they headed to the airport that Saturday afternoon to pick up Jere and Lauri. He was so excited and they were happy to see him, touch him, and share the next five days with him.

The short week was filled with long chats, family dinners, Uno card games with all the adult kids and Ivan, Lasse on the couch watching over all of them. He tried to eat; he fought to eat when

Lauri made smoked salmon for Lasse. He said it was the best he'd ever eaten and it was because it was made with love.

Jere and Lauri had made plans for Tuesday, which was Lasse's chemo day. Michelle put Lasse in the car but had forgotten his numbing cream for his port and she went back in the house. She grabbed the cream and paused in the dining room where Jere and Lauri were sitting.

"Look, I want you to understand where we are right now; you have to know," she said with a little sob. "The doctor said we aren't talking about years anymore," she sniffed hard, then exhaled, "we're talking about months. He doesn't believe that Lasse will live more than a few months." She exhaled deeply as she had said what they needed to know.

Gentle Jere nodded and replied, "Yes. Lasse has said to me last night that it is only months."

"No, he did not say this to me," Lauri said, shaking his head. "Maybe we could skip the family dinner and have time to chat alone with Lasse tonight."

"Of course, we will arrange that. I have to go – let me know if there is anything I can do for either of you." She hurried back to the car and kept her emotions under control so Lasse would not be upset.

"We're going to be late." He was grumpy and stated his dissatisfaction.

"No, we're not, Lover. I'll get you there on time." And she pulled right up to the door of the grandiose cancer treatment center, put Lasse in a wheel chair, leaving him inside the warm foyer while she parked the car and traipsed back to him through the salted, icy sidewalks.

His infusion went smoothly but before it was complete Lasse needed the restroom. Michelle held him around the waist and steered his infusion tower as she guided him down the hall. She helped him get seated on the toilet and then pulled the door closed to give him privacy but stood right outside for when he needed her. She thought she heard him call her name and she quickly opened the door.

"Did you call my name, Lover?" she inquired tensely.

"No. That was my ass," he reported wryly while Michelle got the giggles over his gas bubbles. She adored him completely.

When they returned to his infusion cubicle Marah surprised them with a visit. She brought a cold protein shake for Lasse and a hot coffee for Michelle. She loved on them and encouraged them, even though seeing Lasse in this weakened condition broke her heart. She had kindly brought a huge tray of Dorothy Lane Market's famous Killer Brownies to the nursing staff and thanked them profusely for taking such great care of Lasse. Again, both Lasse and Michelle were so abundantly blessed with love and kindness; Marah was like their own daughter and they loved and appreciated her as such.

At 7:00 the morning of February 22, 2018 Jere and Lauri hugged Lasse tightly. None of the three men said much, a few whispers between them and then Lasse ordered them to get in the car before they were late for their international flight.

Michelle began her normal chatting to try to ease the heavy emotions as she put the car in reverse and backed out of the driveway.

"I am sorry, Michelle," Jere said tightly and putting a hand up, "I cannot speak right now." She just wanted to sob to see gentle, kind Jere struggling to maintain his composure. Lauri sat silently in the back seat looking out the window, none of them saying much on their ride to the airport. She hugged them and watched as they left the security check, heading to their gate. Then she hurried back home to Lasse. They would pray their way out of this valley.

"Bambina, make some coffee, little Finnish cups, and bring some Grand Marnier. We will have café normali." He sat tucked in blankets on the couch, reading on his iPad.

Michelle made the coffee and brought the orange liquor in whiskey glasses. They sipped, he spoke of trips to Tunisia and Afghanistan, she refilled the liquor at his order, and she adored him more. He showed her a particular mountain range he had traveled and she asked, "What did you do there, Lover?"

"I solved problems." Seriously, could he be any cooler? Her own James Bond/Clint Eastwood. He was a sexy, skinny beast. But there was something more that needed said.

"Whatever you have done, you have done for good, Lasse. And if needed, God forgives." He would never give her details and she never asked but she sat on the floor next to the couch as he showed the map of the mountains, watching him, loving him, adoring all of the man he was.

# CHAPTER SEVENTEEN

No matter the right turns they tried to make, all seem to go to hell before they could even get going. Lasse had bloody stools, he couldn't eat, his abdomen was swelling, the pain from the lung surgery in August was constant, his blood pressure was low, and he was losing weight. He was 164 pounds fully clothed and wearing Timberland boots. Michelle calculated that he must be in the 150's at this point. She tried valiantly to feed him, even the protein shakes she had ordered by the case to be delivered to the house, anything to help him gain weight and regain some strength.

March began with a hopeful meeting with Dr. Norvak, who planned a colonoscopy to see about the bleeding. He was kind, caring, and honest. March 2nd was the day scheduled for a paracentesis, where fluid was drawn out of Lasse's very tight abdomen. Seven pounds of fluid was drained away. He could breathe, he could eat something. He had chemo the following week, along with IV fluids, which seemed to pool right to his abdomen, so again paracentesis was performed. A spiraling nightmare of being dehydrated, IV fluids, and then paracentesis commenced.

March 11th Lasse pushed himself to his very limits with the bowel prep and fasting before his scheduled colonoscopy in the morning. The details of that day were burned into Michelle's memory as some of the worst suffering; both of them were traumatized. She helped him with all of it and wept as he endured the agony. His great suffering was her great suffering. All he endured, she endured. "My precious husband! My precious husband! God!!! Please help my Lasse!"

Dr. Norvak performed the colonoscopy and even with Lasse's very low blood pressure he had to administer some anesthesia or Lasse would not have been able to withstand the exam.

"There is something in the colon that I biopsied. It is most likely cancer as you have already had that diagnosis. I'm sorry." He was kind and he was direct.

Michelle got Lasse dressed and ordered a wheelchair to get him to the car. He was not able to stand. She again had to practically carry him from the car and into the house. He was so dehydrated and weak, she called Dr. Brown's office. He was in the Bahamas but his Physician's Assistant admitted Lasse to the hospital for nutrition and hydration.

Immediately the hospitalist doctors came to evaluate Lasse.

"Mr. Paivola, do you have a living will?"

"He lives; that's our deal," Michelle stated as she always had when they were asked that question.

"Mr. Paivola do you want a DNR signed? Do Not Resuscitate? In your condition, should you have a heart attack, if we performed

CPR we would most likely break your ribs and sternum and you wouldn't live long anyway. Would you like a DNR?"

Lasse pierced Michelle with his brilliant blue eyes, "I am sorry, Bambina." Then he looked at the doctor and said, "Yes, I want the DNR."

What the fuck? Michelle thought, fine, I will take you home and make you live anyway. DNR, please; no need because it isn't going to happen. Lasse took her hand. He was serious and she was sure he would live.

Then Lasse was asked if he had pain and he answered that he did. He was given morphine. It didn't stop the pain but it did make him loopy. Then he was given all the strongest pain medicines and each time Michelle would explain that Lasse didn't take those medicines because they caused his bowel not to function. She insisted each nurse read the notes in his chart that stated he did not take narcotic drugs. Lasse was also given a new medicine that was administered to every patient on that floor. The nurse listened to all Michelle explained and she said, "You might want to decline this particular drug because it causes constipation." Michelle was livid but grateful. Dear God, all of this was wrong. Lasse was incoherent and sleeping except when finally, after all the narcotic drugs, his gut would not function. That is when the fecaloid vomiting began once again, the nightmare from Cleveland had reoccurred. Lasse was puking shit and Michelle was rotating the buckets and cleaning his face and mouth; only now she had to hold him up because he could not get himself up. She was carrying him through hell. And Michelle fought all the doctors to get him off the pain medicines so he could think clearly.

Once Lasse was coherent, back to using Tylenol for his pain, she had bathed him and brushed his hair, tucked him back into his hospital bed, he took her hand and said weakly, "Bambina, I would not be alive if it weren't for you. You saved my life."

"Lasse, I would do anything for you." They were looking into each other's souls, her green eyes fierce and his blue eyes still shining. She was sure he would live, he had to; he wasn't so sure.

Michelle's cell phone rang; it was Dr. Norvak. He called to tell them that there was no cancer in Lasse's colon. That tumor was benign. Oh, the relief that flooded them both. And the doubt that filled Michelle; two and a half years earlier that should have been the same finding. She never believed Lasse even had cancer in the first place. But after all the chemotherapy and CT and PET scans and radiation, of course he did now.

Michael, Christopher, Marah, and Ivan came to sit with them for hours, sometimes being there altogether, sometimes taking turns. But they were always there. Michelle ran to the hospital cafeteria while they were there but returned to find Lasse being held in Michael's arms while Christopher held the puke bucket. Christopher wiped Lasse's beard with paper towels, helped him to rinse his mouth, and then took a warm cloth and washed his face. Lasse's hair had fallen down into his eyes and Christopher brushed it back with his hand. Michael whispered calming words to Lasse and carefully laid him back on his pillows. The love of their family was immense. Lasse could never forget this tender care and if any a man knew he was loved, it was him.

Two days later the hospitalist doctor came in to inform them that there was nothing more that the hospital could do for Lasse since all he was taking was Tylenol for pain and that he was being discharged. Michelle argued that the man was puking shit and could not even stand without support. Michelle told the doctor that Lasse was scheduled for chemotherapy across the street before noon and the doctor replied, "Mr. Paivola no longer qualifies for chemotherapy. He needs to go home." And just like that they were kicked out of the hospital with a wheelchair and the message to go home and die.

Dr. Brown was perturbed when they saw him for the chemo appointment. Michelle had wheeled Lasse over to the cancer center from the hospital through their connecting walkway.

"They cannot tell you that you can't have chemo – I am your oncologist and if you want to keep trying then we will do all we can!"

"Thank you," Lasse exhaled.

The chemo and immunotherapy infusion was rescheduled for the next day. Lasse, buckled in the passenger side of the car, held a bucket filled with paper towels as Michelle drove carefully through the snow. She prayed as she drove and a song came on the radio that boosted her belief that Lasse would make it, "That's What Faith Can Do". "I've seen miracles just happen," she sang out loud, touching Lasse's arm, willing him to live. He had to live. Of course he would live. If all they had left to hope for was a miracle, then she believed God would provide them with one.

She pulled up to the cancer treatment center and put the car in park while she ran for a wheelchair. She physically picked Lasse up and put him into the wheelchair with his bucket on his lap. She pushed him inside where it was warm and went to park the car. As she ran through the doors towards him, Lasse was once again puking shit into that bucket.

"Oh, Lover!" she cried with despair, holding him as he bowed over the bucket. Someone had brought paper towels to her and she began cleaning Lasse's face. She finally got him upstairs and checked into the infusion center, where they put him in a private room with a hospital bed. He asked her to cover his eyes to escape into sleep while the infusion took place.

A young nurse came into their room. She was sweet and Michelle tried not to hate her as she began her own cancer story. "My dad died last year from cancer. The one thing we need to keep in mind is that someday we're all going be together again, after we die."

"That's right," Michelle nodded. But he is not going to die, her mind declared vehemently. He does not die. He will not die. Lasse Paivola shall live and not die, in Jesus' Name. He will live. He will not die. He cannot die. He won't.

The next day brought a paracentesis which caused more dehydration. But Lasse's belly was so swollen and painful, the paracentesis was the only thing that relieved the pressure. They called the fluid that was removed, "malignant ascites" and said it was cancerous, too. All they knew was that they were in a shit storm of trouble and could not find their way out.

Lasse's blood pressure was lower than ever and he could not fight to stay conscious while standing. Michelle did carry him in through the door from the car, hardly keeping him from passing out until she could get him to the couch. He told her to get him to the toilet and she took him but he nearly passed out sitting there.

"Lasse! Wake up! We have to get you to the bed right now! Come on!" she ordered, so filled with fear she was shaking. She scooped him up and he passed out in her arms.

"No! Wake up, Lasse! You will not break your foot!" she shouted at him as his foot turned under his legs. She was filled with the strength she needed to carry him down the hallway to the bed in the spare room. Once prone, he began to regain consciousness.

"Oh dear God, Lasse! You scared me! Are you okay?!"

"I don't know. I don't know," he whispered, shaking his head. "Get me the bucket," he demanded.

Michelle grabbed the bucket and put herself behind Lasse to hold him up as the fecaloid vomiting commenced. Finally she carefully cleaned his face and beard, helped him rinse his mouth, and laid him gently on several pillows. They both sighed relief and Michelle kissed his cheeks. She went to rinse the bucket and he called again, "Bucket."

This rotation of puking shit, rinsing buckets, getting Lasse up, and cleaning him up lasted all night long. Neither of them slept. Michelle sat behind Lasse with her arms around him, holding his bucket, wiping his face, and crying out loud to God, "Jesus! Please help him!"

Early in the morning Michelle sent a text to Christopher and Marah. "Would you guys please come over here? There's a new home health nurse coming and we didn't sleep, I don't even know what to say to her because I am so exhausted. Please come." Immediately Christopher and Marah and Ivan were there. Michelle called the on call oncologist and told her everything that had transpired throughout the night. Michelle gave her all of Lasse's vital information, including his very low blood pressure. This was the same doctor who had convinced Lasse of the DNR.

"Well, just give him more Gatorade." That was it. She had no other medical advice.

Christopher and Marah answered the door and took the nurse to the bedroom where Lasse was trying to rest. She took his blood pressure and demanded an ambulance. Michelle explained to her that she had already called the hospital and the on call oncologist had said to give more Gatorade. But the nurse said no way because Lasse was going to die if they did not get him to the hospital right now.

In their small town, the men who were part of the fire and EMS team also went to school with Michael, Christopher, and Marah. One of the guys was Dan Shepherd; he carefully lifted Lasse to the gurney and loaded him into the ambulance. Dan always showed up and their family prayed that God would bless him for all the good he did for others. Ivan watched quietly with wide eyes as his Poppi was taken away by the ambulance.

At the nearest emergency room, which was an inner-city hospital where most visitors were of the gunshot and stabbing variety, the fecaloid vomiting continued. The ER doctor examined Lasse and went to explain the situation to Christopher and Marah. Michelle stayed with Lasse, cleaning him up to protect his dignity as best she could.

"Your father is going to need to get out of here and to the hospital where his own doctors can see him. And he needs an NG tube right away to stop this vomiting."

Lasse was loaded into another ambulance and Michelle rode up front with the driver. His name was Isaiah and he had a long bushy beard with long hair pulled back in a loose ponytail. He was listening to Christian music and he and Michelle began to discuss faith in Jesus. He promised that he would pray for Lasse.

Lasse was taken to the ICU and it was more than an hour before Michelle was allowed to go back to his room. She was frantic as she waited in a small and crowded room. She was delirious from lack of sleep and sick with worry.

"Lover," she breathed as she bent over his beloved face. He had the NG tube and he was resting. He nodded slowly and barely lifted a hand, too weak to speak. A knock on the door and there was Isaiah, the ambulance driver.

"May we come in and pray with you?"

"Oh, yes! Yes, please!"

That young man had brought two other EMS people who held hands with Lasse and Michelle and prayed healing and protection and life for Lasse. It was amazing and beautiful and filled them both with strength and hope. Michelle thanked them effusively. Oh dear God, she was so grateful. Keep sending Your angels, Heavenly Father, she prayed.

A nurse entered, "Mr. Paivola, we have been ordered to give you a 500ml enema. You don't have to get up, just let us help you take care of this."

They had taken an x-ray and wanted to clear his bowel. This was a tough process considering his condition but it was necessary and helpful. Once completed the nurse and Lasse decided another 500ml enema was needed. He felt so much better having his system cleaned out.

A hospitalist doctor came by to give them the results of blood tests. Lasse's CEA was 39, incredibly half of what it was; the chemotherapy and immunotherapy were working. Lasse was going to make it. Michelle quoted Winston Churchill, "If you're going through hell, keep going." They were going to keep going.

Night came, Lasse slept, and Michelle nodded off in the chair beside his bed, her hand on his leg.

"Michelle, wake up." Lasse ordered at 2:00 am.

"What's the matter, Lover?" she asked groggily but ready to jump into action if he needed something.

"There was this black thing beside me and it was trying to pull my port out and I said, 'Get away from me in Jesus' Name!' and it left!"

"Oh my gosh, Lasse! Oh my gosh! It was death and you said the right thing to make it leave in Jesus' Name!"

"Get the phone. I want to make a video for Finland."

Michelle held the phone and recorded him as he spoke to all the Finnish family. He was more alert than he had been in days but still weak. He assured them that though things had been very tough, his CEA was down by half and the chemo was shrinking the tumors in his lungs and that he would be okay. They shared this through the WhatsApp group Lasse had been using with them so they would all know he was okay.

He was still shaken up by the event and Michelle searched for a video of a song by Zach Williams, "Fear is a Liar". She played it for him and he calmed. He slept a little then whispered, "Play the fear song again." She played it for him again and he felt peaceful.

Early in the morning a different hospitalist doctor came with a handful of interns. They said their good morning greetings and then discussed Lasse's case as if he wasn't present. The eager, young interns were very interested in his disease status and asked all kinds of questions that left both Lasse and Michelle feeling deflated.

Dr. Aaron Peters asked Lasse, "Mr. Paivola, have you had a bowel movement this morning?"

"No."

"Well, have you passed gas?"

"No."

Michelle interjected, "He had two 500ml enemas last night and three ice chips since then with an NG tube sucking out the contents of his stomach. He doesn't have anything left to pass."

"That's still not good, not good at all." Dr. Peters pinched his bottom lip between his finger and thumb. He then took his entourage and moved on to another room.

It was as if death came right into the room and took the hope right out of both Lasse and Michelle.

A knock on the door and it was Isaiah. He had returned with two different EMS team members and they were there to pray once again over Lasse.

If ever there was a visible spiritual battle for one man's life, it could be seen in light and darkness taking turns entering that room. Life and death took turns fighting for Lasse. Isaiah returned a third time to pray over Lasse and they were both so eternally grateful.

That afternoon Michelle took out some paper and wrote a prayer for Lasse. "Heavenly Father, We know You are sending streams of refreshment in the Valley of Baca. This is tough, this is dangerous, but we are buffered by You. Show us Your pillar of cloud by day and Your pillar of fire by night. We know You don't leave us nor forsake us. I am so afraid but You told us to fear no evil because You are with us. You know all the healing that Lasse needs. You have healed his soul; please heal his body. By Your Name – YHWH – Yeshua- Jesus – please bring healing and restoration to Lasse's entire being. Protect him from evil and mistakes. Bless him with Your shalom. Of all the grace and Your goodness that has been given to me, please give to him. Lasse shall live and not die in the Name of Jesus! Please cause all of his body to return to good health and to function the way You created it to. Thank You for blessing me with Lasse. You have brought me the one my soul loves. Thank You. Having done all, help us to stand and may we see the salvation of our God and Your blessing in the land of the living. Every praise to You, Heavenly Father. In Jesus' Name I pray all these things."

After a couple of days Lasse was moved to the ICU step down unit, a cot was brought in for Michelle because she would not leave him. The crew of rotating interns took their turns giving their hopeless opinions and even started nipping and biting at every ounce of hope Lasse and Michelle had left. They were like filthy, attacking hyenas, mocking with their vicious words of death.

"You need to understand," one young woman said, stressing the word need, "that Mr. Paivola is not going to live much longer."

Michelle, barely able to keep her emotions under control, said through clenched teeth, "Listen, his CEA is in half, the tumors in his lungs are shrinking, and the chemotherapy is working. He had a series of bad events and he is dehydrated and can't eat because of the ascites. He is getting better."

"The ascites is malignant," the intern said with a blank look on her face. "You have to prepare for what's ahead."

"We know that," Michelle stated tightly. "We know where we stand. If Steve Jobs and all his money could not cure cholangiocarcinoma, dear God, we know!"

A young male intern came to practice his bedside manner of delivering bad news and said, "You need to understand that he is going to die."

"Listen to me, we know where we stand. We get it. If Steve Jobs and all his money could not cure this cancer, we know where we stand. But you," she shouted, "do not have the right to take someone's hope away. There's a fine line between hope and denial but you still do NOT have the right to take our hope away! Get the fuck out of our room! What kind of doctor do you intend to be anyway? This is a Christian hospital and it should be for helping people to live, not constantly talking them into dying!" The young man looked stricken at Michelle's defensive onslaught and he quietly left the room. They were trying to kill Lasse by getting him to give up and she would fight every last one of them.

None of the hospitalists believed Lasse would live, but they would not give up hope. He had promised he would walk through it and she had promised to carry him. They weren't giving up. Michelle had ardently vowed to Lasse, "I promise to help you live but I will not help you die." She would fight off each of these demonic hyenas that were trying to make Lasse give up, go home, and die.

Dr. Bartholomew's assistant, Britta, came to see Lasse and said, "Oh, Mr. Paivola, don't you worry. We have seen far worse ileus than what you're experiencing and people get better from that; you're going to be fine." Again, light and dark, life and death kept coming into the room.

Dr. Patel, the infectious disease doctor, came and told Lasse to keep strengthening himself because there was nothing wrong with his organs, the chemo was working, his heart was strong. He said, "The reason you keep passing out is because you have been lying in bed so long. Keep getting up little by little and your body will strengthen. You are going to be okay, Sir!"

Michael, Christopher, Marah, and Ivan came to take turns sitting with Lasse. They brought pizza to share but kept it in one of the private waiting rooms and not in front of Lasse. Michael and Christopher stayed in the room with Lasse while Michelle went to visit with Marah and Ivan.

Ivan straddled Michelle's legs, sitting on her lap, and munched on a crust of pizza. "Granny," he paused but bravely asked what was worrying him, "is Poppi going to die?"

"He might, Ivan." That was the first time Michelle could admit it. She was always direct with her sons and with her grandson. "But, Ivan, you know when Poppi goes to his boat, you miss him, right?"

"Yeah."

"Do you love him any less while he is gone?"

"No."

"Do you forget about him?"

"No."

"It's like that when we go to heaven, too, Buddy. We don't love each other any less and we miss each other until we are together again. Okay?"

"Yeah."

It had been days since Michelle had showered or even changed her clothes so she agreed with Lasse that she would go home and be gone just a couple of hours. She left early, before dawn, so she could be back before the hospitalists came on their rounds.

"Heavenly Father!" she shouted in the car while driving north on I-75. "Your Word says that Your arm is not too short to save but our sins cut You off from helping us. Is there anything I am doing wrong that would keep You from helping Lasse?" Immediately the Bible verses from Proverbs 3 came to her mind. "Trust in the Lord with all your heart and lean not on your own understanding. In all your ways acknowledge Him and He shall direct your paths." She sighed another prayer, "Okay, God, what do I need to do? Show me what to do to help Lasse. Please."

As Michelle quickly showered she decided she would call the hospital in Cleveland and get Lasse transported there as soon as possible. She tried to reach Dr. Miller who had started the colon cancer battle but ended up speaking with the on-call doctor. "Yes, we will take Mr. Paivola immediately; he will always be our patient. We will arrange the transportation but there is no cure for him so we will just be doing palliative care but we can help his ileus and make his life more comfortable."

Michelle was on a mission to get Lasse where there were experts and not a bunch of idiots wearing white coats pretending to be doctors. She called her sister, Heather, while she drove back to the hospital. "That sounds like the best decision, Sister! Get him back to Cleveland! That Viking is not going to be taken down by a gas bubble!" Heather always had the most creative way to encourage others.

When Michelle entered Lasse's room he was on the phone with his best buddy, John Harkrader. "I promise, John," Lasse said, "Here is Michelle, ask her." He handed the phone to Michelle.

"Hi John," she said.

"Look, I have spent years hunting with Lasse and talking about everything on earth but I never made sure he has Jesus. I cannot let him leave this world without being saved."

"John, I promise you that Lasse has Jesus. I wouldn't let him leave without Jesus either. But he isn't going to leave us just yet, okay? Thank you for making sure, Friend."

She was anxious to tell Lasse about her prayers and speaking with the doctor at the hospital in Cleveland but she gave Lasse time to tell her about his call with John.

"I asked him why I am going through all this and why isn't God helping and he told me, 'Trust in the Lord with all your heart and lean not on your own understanding.' That is what he said and then I looked on my tray they brought in this morning and that same Bible verse was there, 'Trust in the Lord with all your heart.' And John said the same words to me."

"Lasse, God said the same words to me in the car. I asked Him if there was anything I am doing that is keeping Him from helping us and He whispered into my soul, 'Trust in the Lord with all your heart and lean not on your own understanding'! And then I called the hospital in Cleveland and they said they can help if you have a bowel obstruction – which this place has said you do not have any kind of complete obstruction. Dr. Miller is going to call us back later and we can get out of here; they will arrange it all!"

Lasse weakly pumped his fist in the air and declared, "We're traveling then!" He was ready to get out of there and back to Cleveland, too.

Dr. Peters entered the room while Michelle was massaging Lasse's legs because they were aching and numb. She held his foot to her chest and rubbed up and down his legs, working mentholated ointment into his feet at his request.

"Oh, I wish I had a wife who would massage my feet like that; I don't mean I want your wife," he blundered, chuckling, "I mean I want a wife like her!"

"Yeah," Lasse muttered a reply.

"Do you massage your husband's legs like that all the time?"

"No, just when he feels like crap and asks me to do it; I'd do anything for him." Michelle loathed this young man.

"Mr. Paivola, have you had a bowel movement? Passed any gas?"

"No."

"That's not good. Maybe we should order another enema," Dr. Peters said contemplatively, while again pinching his bottom lip between his forefinger and thumb. "No, that could perforate his bowel, maybe we better not."

Michelle looked at him and thought she would knock him out right there. "Based on what? Why all of a sudden do you think an enema would perforate his bowel? He had two 500ml enemas a few days ago, they helped and he was fine."

Another hospitalist doctor entered the room and he said another enema might help but concurred with Dr. Peters that it might perforate Lasse's bowel.

Michelle was exhausted and exasperated but determined to get Lasse out of there.

"We have contacted our hospital in Cleveland and they are making arrangements to transport Lasse there."

The doctors began conferring with one another when Michelle's phone rang. It was Lasse's colon cancer doctor, Dr. Miller, who had performed his surgeries in Cleveland. Michelle still hated him but was clinging to that call like a lifeline.

"Mrs. Paivola, I am sorry to hear that Mr. Paivola is in such bad condition," he stated in his curt, German accent. "I cannot take him as my patient because I only do curative surgeries. Someone else can take him for palliative care but I cannot. I have read his online charts, Mrs. Paivola, and your husband is going to die. You have to understand that. He is going to die. This is going to kill him."

He got all of that out before she had time to say anything. Calmly she said, "I understand. Your on-call doctor said he would take him as his patient."

"Yes, he can come, he can always come here; he will always be our patient. But I cannot take him because I do not do those kinds of surgeries. I am sorry, Mrs. Paivola."

Unbelievable, Michelle thought. He doesn't want Lasse to ruin his rock star surgeon reputation. He won't help him because he can't fix him. He won't even help him. She would store her rage for Dr. Miller for another day and it would boil for a long time. She would hate him for a very long time.

Mike and Heather came from Kentucky to spend the day and were waiting in the hall while all of this chaos took place.

"What did Dr. Miller say, Michelle?" Lasse asked.

"He said you can come to Cleveland but you'll have to see another doctor. He can't see you because he only does curative surgeries."

Lasse understood what Dr. Miller meant but what Michelle refused to relay. "Okay. I want to be unhooked from all of this and go home."

"Lasse, wait," Michelle pleaded desperately. She got on her knees and took his hand. "Lasse, please, they can help you. You don't have any complete obstruction; they can fix this. Your chemo is working, your CEA is in half, and the tumors in your lungs are shrinking. Lover, please. Dr. Bartholomew, Britta, Dr. Patel, they all believe you can make it. Please."

"No. I am done with them playing with my life. I want to go home."

Michelle put her head on Lasse's stomach and he put his hand in her hair. "Lover, please. Lasse, you are not lost to God and I am not lost to God. But we will be lost to each other," she said thickly, tears spilling out and onto his blankets.

"But only for a little while," Lasse said quietly but firmly. "I will go home." Lasse had made up his mind and was the ruler of his own life. These idiots were no longer going to play these games with him.

"Fine, Lasse. I will take you home and make you live." She opened the door for Heather and Mike to come in. Mike pulled up a chair to Lasse's bedside and Heather took Michelle to the cafeteria for a meal and a visit.

"Make him live, Sister. You can do it. Just get him out of here where they don't have a clue how to help him. You kept Old Petey alive for years!" Heather was referring to a sixteen year old dog that had been dropped off at Michelle's farm decades earlier that she nursed back to health and vitality after he was declared nearly dead.

Mike, always the joker, was stern-faced when the women returned. Michael, Christopher, and Marah had also arrived and Lasse made his decision known to them as well. Dr. Peters came back into the room and Lasse said, "If I was in Finland I would fly to Belgium, they would investigate my status, I'd sign a form, and they would give me the pill. How does it work here?"

Dr. Peters was ready with a reply as this was the outcome he had sought. Finally, they understood. "Hospice is our euthanasia here. We will send some hospice companies in and you can decide which one you want to help you. This is the right decision, Mr. Paivola."

Lasse pointed to Mike and said, "I can't see prolonging this if I can't go hunting any more with that guy."

Mike looked down at the floor and said, "If that's what you want to do, Boss." Michelle seethed, and the rest of the family fought back the tears.

Michelle did not say a word. So, the hospice companies would give their sales pitch and they could decide who got their business. Wow. That's our euthanasia. Incredible. She never addressed another word to Dr. Peters but she vowed she would kill him with her bare hands, she would physically attack him, and then stomp him to death. She imagined it repeatedly and had murdered him many times in her mind.

Lasse asked to see each family member alone and he spoke his heart to them. They all kept their shared words with Lasse to themselves, treasured moments with a man they loved and were losing. He never said anything he didn't mean and he would make sure they all followed through with his wishes.

He ordered Michelle to get the hospice companies in immediately so they could interview them. "Okay, fine," she said stonily. "I guess you've always told me, 'You will do it or you will cry and do it,' so I will cry and do this. But you are going to live, Lasse; I will make you live."

Monday, April 2, 2018, after a stormy afternoon with a tornado warning that delayed their ambulance, Lasse was unhooked from all their machines and was heading home. Dr. Patel had heard about Lasse's decision and came to say goodbye. "Oh, my friend! I am struck!" he exclaimed as he threw his arm across his chest. "Why?" He tried to send Lasse home with a two week antibiotic but the hospice company nurse told him he knew they didn't do antibiotics as that would prolong life.

Britta came and brought Dr. Bartholomew's replacement physician, a retired military doctor who tried to sternly change Lasse's mind. "We won't bar the door if you want to leave but I had a friend who had this same cancer. They found a new chemo for him and he lived another year. It all came back but he got another year." Lasse did not respond. He had made the decision to quit this life and he was sticking to it.

Dr. Brown, the oncologist, stopped by the hospital room just before departure and said to Michelle, "Don't give him the morphine; it will only constipate him more. I am prescribing a drug that makes paralyzed people have bowel movements. Get him to take that and he will be okay."

Michelle had ordered a bedside commode and a heated mattress pad online to be delivered that day so Lasse would be as comfortable as possible. She wanted him warm. Christopher was at their house when the ambulance arrived after 10pm and he helped to get Lasse tucked into one of the twin beds in the guest room. "Mom, this is what he wants and we will honor that." Christopher was the most honorable kind of man and he loved Lasse without question.

Michelle's mouth tightened and she said, "He is not going to die. We will make him live."

Lasse had agreed to keep the NG tube so he would not spend his last few days with fecaloid vomiting and the hospice company had sent suction equipment. Christopher helped Michelle get it set up on a bedside table and made sure everything was secure for the night.

Michelle knew her battle was with Lasse now and she'd never won a battle with him. He was the king of her life and she'd always done as he said. She got the frankincense, prayed over him, kissed him, and fell asleep on the twin bed beside him. He slept and so did she but she prayed continually for help to stop this train she had no control over.

In the morning there were calls to all of his children in Finland and to his sister. He asked each one if there was anything he needed to make right with them and he asked their forgiveness. He asked his children to apologize to their mother for him. He did all he could to make things right between God and himself and between himself and any living person. He told them he had made this decision and that he loved them. They respected him and his choice.

Michelle was determined to get Dr. Brown's laxative medicine into Lasse but he refused. "Lasse, you know you can live, you can make it! All of your own doctors say you can make it! You are not supposed to be dying!" She tried, dear God, how she tried.

The hospice nurse was a spunky woman with a red convertible Volkswagen. "You're doing a fine job with him," she declared. "I don't think I'll need to stop in every day but if you need me at any time I will be here."

"That's fine, thank you," Michelle responded automatically. "I have been doing all his care and I want to do it. I managed all of his care with the ileostomy; I can do anything he needs. And all of our family is here to help, too."

"Alright, well, you just give me a call any time, day or night, if you need anything. I think it will be around seven days, that's how long it will take."

Ah, that's how long it will take to dehydrate someone to death, Michelle thought. Fucking fantastic. She thought it was one thing to tuck grandma in the bed when it was her time to go but quite another to dehydrate a human being to death. She knew this was all wrong and she was so against Lasse's decision.

The hospice nurse explained how to administer morphine if Lasse needed it and the special box filled with all kinds of pain medication for the last few hours that was to be kept in the fridge.

Michael, Christopher, Marah, and Ivan were in the house all of the time, taking turns sitting with Lasse just to be near him for as long as possible. Ivan brought his airplane neck pillow and gave it to Poppi. He leaned in close to Lasse and swapped sniffs with him, just the way they had always done.

"I am praying for you, Poppi."

"Thank you, Boy."

In the first couple of days Michelle had all the hope that Lasse would change his mind. She began taking care of laundry and dishes and gave him a small bell to ring if he needed her immediately. He would ring that bell and she would shake her head, knowing that bossy man still had life in him. She would be at his side within seconds with a urinal and to plead with him to take ice chips to which she had drizzled a little honey, hoping it would give him energy.

Lasse spoke quietly and seriously to Michelle, "After I am gone, you are the only person who will see my body. Do you understand?"

"Yes." When was he going to put the brakes on this death sentence? He could change his mind; why wouldn't he just fight to live?

John Harkrader came. He hugged Michelle at the door and then marched himself to Lasse's bedside. He bent over Lasse and scooped him up in a bear hug, Lasse cried silently and beat his fist on John's back. "Brother," Lasse whispered. John sat in a chair beside Lasse and they talked a long time; Michelle had closed the door.

When John left the room he asked, "Michelle, can you come back here for a second?"

They went into Lasse and Michelle's bedroom and she watched as this giant of a man tried to gather his words with tears streaming down his face. "I don't think I'll ever see him again in this life."

"John, he is not going to die. I will not let him die. He is not supposed to die yet." Michelle was adamant, lifting her chin, her nostrils flaring in her determination.

"I think he is ready to go."

"He doesn't care. I don't know why he is doing this. It is not his time to go."

"He does care," John whispered with passion. "He cares so much that is why he is going."

"I do not understand," Michelle said but she refused to cry. That man was not going to die and that was that.

"Listen to me, he wants to be cremated and have his ashes taken to Finland and I want to go whenever you decide to take them. And you do not have to take them now; there's no hurry. You can take them when you're ready. It can be next year if you want."

Michelle wished he would shut up. Just because John was ready to agree with Lasse did not mean this was true. It was not time for Lasse to die. It was not. She knew John loved Lasse and would do whatever the man wished. Which of them wasn't in that same position with Lasse?

People began dropping off food. Michelle didn't think they needed anything but as the family stayed it was so wonderful to have something to feed all of them without planning or cooking.

Mike and Heather came. Mike took up John's chair beside Lasse's bed. Lasse said to him, "You lost that knife I brought you from Finland!"

"Oh, yeah, I did. Remember we were both riding on my ATV and we stopped to eat lunch and then it was gone. We looked for that knife for hours. I'm sorry, Boss, I never found it. Man, I hate that I lost that thing. I'm sorry; I didn't know it still bothered you." Mike didn't know what else to say to Lasse but he explained the entire story to Michelle as Lasse drifted back to sleep. Mike stayed by Lasse's side and Michelle would peek in to see if either needed anything. Mike was just sitting quietly holding Lasse's hand as he slept. What a brother and such a very good man.

Sunday, April 8th, Lasse woke up and said with exasperation, "I'm not dead? Why can't I die?"

"Because you are not supposed to be dying, Lasse! What are you going to say to God when you show up, 'Reporting early for duty, Sir,'?" She was so angry because he refused the laxative medicine and hardly took any ice chips as not to prolong his life. "I asked the hospice nurse why and she said usually the person has something else they have to do. You have not apologized to me for leaving me before it is time!"

"I'm sorry," Lasse said sullenly. He just wanted to get this dying behind him.

Michelle gritted her teeth, "I forgive you but I am still mad at you, Lasse." She thought for a moment. "You never reached Jonte about the van. He will need to know you have forgiven him."

"Get me paper." Michelle brought a pen and a card so Lasse could write to Jonte. He was the son of Lasse's best friend in Finland and some things had gone awry with the sale of Lasse's van a few years earlier. Lasse had forgiven Jonte but had not been able to get in contact with him. He wrote a few words in Finnish to Jonte and Michelle promised she would hand deliver it to him when she took Lasse's ashes to Finland.

"Do not worry about my ashes, Michelle. This body is just a piece of shit. When you take my ashes to Finland, just put them in a cardboard box with a weighted stone. Do not spend any money on this. You can ship them by FedEx if needed. And if you can't get them to Finland then the Atlantic is just as well."

Michelle clamped her jaw shut and her nostrils flared slightly. She took a couple of deep breaths to calm herself. He was not giving up the giving up. He was the one man she did not boss.

Lasse said to Michelle as she bathed him tenderly in the bed, "The first six months will be the worst."

"That's what you think, Lasse, but I will be without you for the rest of my life. Please, stop this. Drink some water. Please. Have some ice chips."

Lasse closed his eyes in reply. Later when he woke up he looked at Michelle with the happiest smile. "Every time I have ever seen you I have thought you are so beautiful!"

"Oh, my love," she said, treasuring his sweet words. How could she get him to change his mind about dying?

Lasse was not in a lot of pain and never once asked for morphine. He kept his senses together very well even through the dehydration. But he was exhausted of the dying process. Michelle was sure he would become bored with it, give up, and start letting her feed him.

"Why am I still alive?" he asked.

"Because we are all praying for you, Lasse. Ivan got on his knees and begged God to shake the whole earth if that is what it will take to heal you!"

"Tomorrow I want you to show him the scene from "The Lord of the Rings" where Frodo doesn't go back to the Shire but he goes with Gandalf. Then I want you to bring him here to me so I can talk with him."

The next day Michelle did as Lasse ordered, of course she did. He was the boss of their family. When she showed Ivan the clip of Frodo saying goodbye to his friends, Michelle asked him, "Ivan, do you understand why Poppi wants you to see this?"

Ivan didn't speak but nodded his head. "Poppi wants to tell you something now, Buddy."

Christopher and Marah gathered around Lasse's bed as he took Ivan's hand. "Boy," Lasse began with a tired voice, "everything wears out, even this pillow you gave me is someday going to wear out. I am worn out. Do you understand? I want you to stop praying that Poppi will get healed and pray that I go to heaven with Jesus instead. Understand? I love you but I am worn out."

Ivan did not crumple or cry but he did leave the room in a hurry. A few minutes later he came to Lasse's bedside and they sniffed each other as they always had instead of kissing. "Love you, Poppi."

"Love you, Boy."

April 10th was the anniversary of their wedding in Finland. There is a quote by C.S. Lewis, "The pain I feel now is the happiness I had before; that's the deal." If they had never known true love and joy, the coming separation would not be so agonizing. But it was worth it.

That night Michelle slept on the twin bed with Lasse. He kept his hand on her and she wrapped her arm around his waist but did not want to make him uncomfortable. He woke up and said, "Bambina! The keepers said the wine and honey have been ordered but I can stay with you for three more weeks if I want!"

"The keepers? Do you mean like the watchers in Daniel; the angels?"

He was excited that she understood. "Yes! They said I can stay with you for three more weeks if I want!"

"Oh, Lasse, please stay with me, please don't leave me!"

Early in the morning Michelle dialed all of Lasse's family in Finland and held the phone for him as he said goodbye to them. It was heart wrenching but incredibly loving and an honor to help him make those calls.

Later that morning, Michelle brought a bucket of warm soapy water and began to wash Lasse from head to toe. She rubbed his body with frankincense and put the menthol ointment on his feet. She trimmed both his fingernails and his toenails; then she filed them smoothly, something she had never done before. Praying for healing, Michelle bent over Lasse and kissed his lips, then his cheeks, she kissed his neck, and his chest, and his belly, she pressed kisses on his hands and his groin, his legs, and his feet. She imagined that his mother had treated him the same way on the day of his birth seventy-one years earlier in a Finnish sauna. Finally, she wrapped him in a blue and green towel that had belonged to his father.

When Lasse's legs would cramp from dehydration Michelle would sit on the end of the bed and lift them one at a time onto her shoulders while she massaged the Charlie horse away. He said, "Bambina, you are so tough. My mother would be so proud of you for all you have gone through and all you have done for me." She cherished every word. Why? Why did he insist on this?

"Lasse, I am honored to take care of you as only your mother has. You are everything to me." She paused thinking contemplatively, "Birth is a painful and messy business and death seems to be that way, too." Then she whispered, "You are so loved, Lasse."

"I told you that I love you 100,000 times but you never believed me, Michelle." His blue eyes were still bright and determined to make her believe him.

"I believe you, I do! Please do not leave me, Lasse, please, I love you, I need you," she sobbed.

"You're the boss now, Bambina." She didn't want to be the boss; she wanted him for every day of the rest of her life. But she would wear that title along with Mrs. Lasse Paivola. She was his wife forever and no separation would change that commitment.

Michelle had the Gospel of John playing in Finnish for Lasse. It was calming to hear the Bible in his mother tongue and to listen to the words of Jesus promise eternal life to all who believe in Him. The dearest thing Lasse said to Michelle was that he would pray for her when he was with Jesus.

On the afternoon of April 11th the hospice nurse returned and Lasse asked her to remove his NG tube. She said it might be uncomfortable but it would be quick. Marah sweetly held Lasse's hand while the nurse removed the NG tube.

"I can see how much your family loves your husband," she said as she was leaving. "I am sorry, but it won't be much longer now."

Lasse's breathing became raspy and they would lift him up higher on the pillows. He weighed less than 140 pounds. Marah slid her arm under Lasse's torso and lifted him by herself onto the pillows and she quietly said, "I think this is what they call the death rattle, Michelle."

"No, I think he is just having trouble breathing with a sore throat from it being so dry. We have to change his mind about this."

"Michelle, he seems pretty committed to dying."

Now that the NG tube was gone Michelle kissed and kissed Lasse's lips. He kissed her back with as much effort and will as he could. All their kisses from the first fiery kiss in an elevator in Salt Lake City to these tiny goodbye kisses were love exchanged without words.

Michael stayed late that night and held Lasse's hand for hours. He, too, loved Lasse without question and pleaded with him, "Lasse, stop this fucking dying. I know a guy that can get you IV fluids and we can get you into a hospital tonight." He was feeling the desperation and that this was moving past the point of return. Lasse closed his eyes and gently shook his head no.

When Lasse and Michelle were alone in the house, she pushed the other twin bed next to his. She didn't want to disturb his sleeping since his breathing was ragged by sharing his bed as she had before but she wanted to be next to him. She kissed and kissed him, prayed for healing once again, and lay down beside him. They held hands, fingers interlocked and both of them drifted off to sleep.

Michelle woke to the sound of a loud clap and like someone had shouted, "Now!" Lasse's hand was stiff in hers and she knew immediately that he was gone. She jumped from the bed, turned on the light, and said, "Dear God, Lasse!" She was frantic on the inside, her soul was quivering; but all of her actions were calm. She inhaled deeply and climbed across his body and looked intensely into Lasse's opened eyes.

She gave orders to herself. You will memorize his face. Look at his face. He is peaceful. He is not suffering. Look at his lips, slightly parted in awe. What is he seeing? Look at his eyes. He looks almost happy. His eyes are no longer blue but they look golden. Dear God. My Lasse.

She ran to the computer and stopped the recording of the Gospel of John and played a praise song instead. "The Name of Jesus Lives On". Michelle took Lasse's hand and raised it with hers in praise. She figured he better be praising Jesus as he entered His presence.

She called Michael, Christopher, and Marah, then she called hospice. She sent text messages to all the family in Finland. She did all of this as though a machine.

Michael and Christopher handled the cremation arrangements and Marah went with them to the funeral home. Ivan stayed with Michelle and they sat on the couch together crying and singing songs to the Lord.

Michelle would spend the next full year pulling her life together and living as the noble lady Lasse required her to be. When times called for her to be tough, she remembered that he had placed her in authority, "You're the boss now, Bambina." She got up, made the bed, went to work, had her meltdowns, and missed Lasse all of the 86,400 seconds of each day. Her next chapters are being written even now. All the necessary things that needed done she did with his motto, "You will do it or you will cry and do it." Just like writing this story.

# EPILOGUE

She sat in a wheelchair in the aisle of a small bookstore, the light behind the dingy windows greyed because of the rain. Michelle's hair had turned from golden blonde to a bright white over these last thirty-five years and it contrasted and complimented the worn out red carpet beneath her. The shell of her body that she wore over her feisty soul was creased and wrinkled; weakened with age. Her green eyes glittered as a beautiful youngish lady came through the door, having closed her umbrella as she entered.

The woman came up to Michelle and stared into her eyes without saying a word. Her hand reached into her trench coat and she pulled out a small album that she handed to Michelle. Michelle's two boney hands reached for the album and she gasped, a small breath escaping in surprise. This album was the story of her life. The woman still said nothing but looked past the shell of the old lady and it seemed, into her soul. And then Michelle remembered; this was a dream she'd had decades ago. Only she had been the youngish lady walking into the bookstore from the rain and she had been the one to hand the album to the old lady.

The front door opened again and as Michelle looked up, the man who entered was not a stranger. Lasse beamed and said, "Bambina, are you ready to go?" He held out his hand to her and she laughed with utmost joy as she put her hand in his; she felt glorious. She stood up from her wheelchair and out of the shell of her wrinkled and worn body. She was young again. Lasse pulled her to himself and kissed her, this time souls truly melded. Beaming he said, "I told you I would always come back to you."

With tears glistening in her green eyes, she replied, "I have missed you, Lover; I waited all these years for you. Take me to Jesus, Lasse." Their fingers intertwined, they stepped together into the Golden Realm.

# AUTHOR'S NOTE:

I have written this story as Lasse ordered me to do. Even from the heavenly realm he is still bossing me. I have laughed, I have sobbed, and I have fallen more in love with my husband than ever before. He knew writing this would accomplish his desire of keeping him alive in my heart every day. He will never be forgotten.

You know, Ernest Hemingway said, "There is nothing to writing. All you do is sit down at a typewriter and bleed." It's so true. While writing the horrors of all that Lasse suffered, that I suffered with him, I had to go back into those rooms and relive it all. I have died twice. This time there was no hope that he would live because I already knew the outcome. This time I didn't have his hand to hold but sat at my computer weeping, sometimes howling, typing out our story, my entire being broken at the core. But Lasse's motto, "You will do it or you will cry and do it," pushed me to get this done. The writing has been like watching your favorite movie for the tenth time. You cry at all the same sappy bits and laugh at all the same lines but each time it is new even as you quote the lines along with the actors.

I'm laying out the same black summer suit with a pencil skirt and polka-dot sleeveless top with a square neckline that I wore to Salt Lake City in August 2001. I am wearing it when I travel tomorrow to stay at the Grand America and ride the elevator where Lasse kissed me, where my soul was fused with his. No, I won't open my heart to another; I could not. I love Lasse beyond reason and he is my one and only forever. He promised he will always come back to me and I promised I will always wait for him. Death does not mean, "cease to exist"; he'll come and I will wait.

Most sincerely, Michelle L. Paivola